POSITIVE THOUGHTS POSITIVE ACTION

Principles for Personal and Professional Success

Arnold Fox, M.D.
Barry Fox, Ph.D.

The **Napoleon Hill** Foundation

JAICO PUBLISHING HOUSE

Ahmedabad Bangalore Bhopal Chennai
Delhi Hyderabad Kolkata Mumbai

Published by Jaico Publishing House
A-2, Jash Chamber, Sir Phirozshah Mehta Road
Fort, Mumbai - 400 001
jaicopub@vsnl.com
www.jaicobooks.com

© 2008 By The Napoleon Hill Foundation

Published in arrangement with
The Napoleon Hill Foundation
1 College Avenue, Wise
Virginia 24293, USA

POSITIVE THOUGHTS POSITIVE ACTION
ISBN 978-81-7992-891-2

First Jaico Impression: 2008

Printed by
Snehesh Printers
320-A, Shah & Nahar Ind. Est. A-1
Lower Parel, Mumbai - 400 013.

CONTENTS

CONTENTS

INTRODUCTION

by Judith Williamson

Beyond Positive Thinking: Putting Your Thoughts into Action by Drs. Arnold and Barry Fox can stand alone or be read as the sequel to their co-authored book *Wake Up! You're Alive*. Both books focus on living a positive lifestyle by using action oriented strategies that assist a person in seeing the abundant side of life. Critics insist that these ideas do not work, but the Fox family is proof that what you focus on you become. After you read the heartfelt stories that fill the book, you can decide whether or not this is how you want to live your life.

In reading this book, I was especially taken with the story of Sally, a survivor of the Nazi concentration camps, who insisted upon keeping a lit candle on her nightstand while she was in the hospital dying of cancer. When asked to explain why this was so important to her, she retold the story of how she managed to stay alive in the camp by completing a ritual with an imaginary candle and saying to herself, "Light always shines in the darkness." This small amount of positive auto-suggestion enabled her to survive the concentration camp and now she believed that the real candle was going to assist her in outliving the cancer. Her small action of lighting a tiny candle and keeping it burning on her nightstand changed her world on the outside, but more importantly it changed her inner world as well. Positive beliefs followed by positive actions create positive results.

In a book entitled *Man's Search for Meaning*, holocaust survivor Viktor Frankl recounts similar stories. He concludes that the ultimate thing a man can control is his attitude, and with this attitude he molds his destiny. Taking the personal initiative that is necessary to control one's attitude, enables a person to advance on life's journey. Viktor Frankl and Drs. Arnold and Barry Fox demonstrate that in order to advance in life, individuals must first take the initiative to do something about it. That "something" is defined as action. Action is said to be the foundation for success in anyone's life, because without action everything else would be of no value.

In defining personal achievement, Dr. Napoleon Hill, author of *Think and Grow Rich* and *Law of Success*, identifies four principles that are the cornerstones of success. They are: definiteness of purpose, going the extra mile, mastermind alliance and applied faith. Knowing about the "Big Four" as he calls these principles is insufficient unless an individual ties them to action. For example, a person must choose a definite major purpose and create an action plan for its achievement. Next, he must practice the habit of going the extra mile. Third, he must organize a mastermind alliance for the purpose of pursuing his definite major purpose, and finally he must open his mind for guidance through applied faith. Without the "action" part of the process an individual would remain a daydreamer with an imaginary candle. But, with the "action" part in place he strikes the match, lights the candle, and inspires himself to more action through the mental illumination that the candle represents to his inner world. This is a simple formula, yet profound in its ramifications — Thought + Action = Success.

Why not create some success rituals for yourself? They could be as simple as lighting a candle, filling a cup to overflowing and noting the abundance, taking a walk and reveling in nature, making lists of positive accomplishments in your life, and always acknowledging a higher power through reflection and prayer.

Drs. Arnold and Barry Fox have made a major contribution to the field of motivational literature with this book. They have documented personal testimonials for the benefit of taking action oriented steps to improve a person's own outlook on life. As all readers of this genre know, the only person you can change is yourself. And, by changing yourself you can become an example to others and thereby to the world. As you read this book, reflect on the little story below, and in doing so let it set your expectation for what is to follow—action wise—in your life.

When I was a young man,
I wanted to change the world.
I found it was difficult to change the world,
so I tried to change my nation.
When I found I couldn't change the nation,
I began to focus on my town.
I couldn't change the town, and as an older man,
I tried to change my family.
Now as an old man,
I realize the only thing I can change is myself,
and suddenly I realize that if long ago
I had changed myself,
I could have made an impact on my family.
My family and I could have made an impact on our town.
Their impact could have changed the nation
and I could indeed have changed the world.

-Unknown Monk, AD 1100

As a great philosopher once said, "Go and do likewise."

Blessings,
Judy Williamson

NOTE TO THE READER

This book is the result of a close collaboration between the two Foxes. The case histories and personal experiences sometimes involve Arnold, sometimes Barry, sometimes both authors. For the sake of convenience and clarity, we use the "I" voice of Arnold Fox, M.D. throughout.

CHAPTER ONE

BEYOND POSITIVE THINKING

"Even if you're on the right track—
you'll get run over if you just sit there."
-Arthur Godfrey

"Positive thinking is a cruel deception." I couldn't believe my eyes when I read this in a letter addressed to "the Drs. Fox" (Barry and I). Some people feel that positive thinking is a 1960s left over. Some feel that it's nice, but has no real effect on our health or lives. Most people, however, agree that our thoughts strongly influence our health and our lives. We've never heard anyone say that positive thinking is a cruel deception.

Generally speaking, public opinion and scientific research support the idea that there is a strong link between mind and body, with events in one affecting the other. There's a whole new branch of medical science, only about a dozen years old, devoted to studying the links between our thoughts and our immune system, blood chemistry, the heart and other parts of the body.[1] Barry and I have written quite a bit about positive thinking and our immune systems, our hearts, our cholesterol, our health and our lives in general. We usually receive a positive reception.

The Reverend Norman Vincent Peale, who is often called "the father of positive thinking," kindly wrote the introduction for one of our books (*Wake Up! You're Alive*). He then printed sections from *Wake Up! You're Alive* in his wonderful magazine called "Plus—The Magazine of Positive Thinking." The article,

---

[1] Psychoneuroimmunology (psycho-neuro-immun-ology).

titled "Believe!" asked, "*Can faith help you restore your health, live joyfully and become a winner?*" The answer, of course, was "*You bet it can. . .*"

Barry and I were quite proud that Dr. Peale excerpted our book for his magazine. We received many favorable comments. One woman left her hospital bed in Minnesota, flying out to Los Angeles for what she called "the thought medicine." While we were busy congratulating ourselves, however, we received a touching letter from a troubled woman in France. She wrote:

> *Dear Drs. Arnold and Barry Fox,*
>
> *I read your article called "Believe." I've also read your book,* Wake Up! You're Alive.
>
> *I used to be a big believer in positive thinking. Now I think it's a big sham. Think you can, and you can? Believe it will happen, and it will? Positive thinking is no better than the "Dr. Goodfeel's Elixir of Health" the medicine men used to peddle before they were run out of town.*
>
> *I have had five pregnancies, each one ending with miscarriage. I received the new treatment from my doctor for the last pregnancy. I really believed it was going to help. I believed with all my heart. I truly believed that we would finally have a baby. I was wrong. Positivity is not enough! Positive thinking is cruel deception.*
>
> *Please reconsider your advice about positive thinking.*

I immediately showed this letter to Barry, the third of my seven children. After reading the letter, Barry agreed that we should reconsider our advice about positive thinking. It's essential, he said, and we want everyone to be a positive thinker, but sometimes it's not enough.

Sugar-Coated Belief

Most of us will agree that negative thoughts can lead to physical disease and emotional distress. What about positive thinking? Does positive thinking counteract negative thinking? Will positive thinking alone improve our physical and emotional health? Can it increase the size of our bank account? The answer is unequivocally, absolutely yes—sometimes.

We can prove that positive thinking is one of the most powerful forces within the human body. Later on, we'll look at many of the exciting studies illustrating the link between our thoughts and our immune system, our heart, our hormones, even our cholesterol level. For now, consider the humble placebo, that "worthless sugar pill" we doctors use to test new drugs. Some of the patients in a study are given the "real thing," the medicine being studied, while others receive a placebo made to look and feel just like the medicine. Patients do not know if they are receiving the medicine or the placebo.

Some medicines work often, some work rarely, but the placebo always works in 30% or more of patients suffering from all kinds of diseases and problems. Sometimes the "sugar pill" has a "cure" rate as high as 60%!

A placebo is a "sugar pill." It's nothing—nothing but the patient's belief that it will work. It's sugar-coated belief. And in countless thousands of studies the placebo has proven that positive thinking is a powerful medicine.

Can positive thinking help you become healthier, live joyfully and be a winner? You bet it can—sometimes. Let's reconsider our advice about positive thinking, Barry said. Let's tell people that positive thinking is like gasoline: A whole tankful won't do much good until we put our foot on the gas pedal and start driving. Positive thinking makes action possible: Action brings our good thoughts to life. Positive thinking, positive action.

Dancing on the Centrifuge

Positive thinking disappointed the French woman who wanted so much to have a baby. What about positive action? I called my friend, Jeff Steinburg, M.D.,F.A.C.O.G., in Encino, California. A specialist in Reproductive Endocrinology and Infertility, Jeff is Director of the Invitro Fertility Program at the AMI Medical Center, and Director of the Encino Fertility Institute. I've known Jeff since he was a kid; his mother was one of my friends back in South Philly. Grown up, Jeff is now one of the nation's top invitrofertilization (test-tube baby) specialists.

After I described this woman's difficulty, Jeff told me: "Arnie, tremendous new discoveries have been made concerning what goes 'wrong' in women who repeatedly miscarry. We used to believe that most times there was either a problem with the fetus, or something wrong with the environment being provided by the mother in which the fetus was to grow. It turns out that we were wrong, that these are rarely the cause of repeated miscarriages.

"The problem, we have discovered, lies in with the interaction between the mother's and father's tissue types. A portion of the father's tissue type, which is also found in the fetus, is normally supposed to 'tell' the mother that a new pregnancy has arrived. Properly informed, the mother's immune system is supposed to become 'tolerant' of the pregnancy. That is, her immune system is supposed to recognize that although the new fetus is 'foreign' to her, it should not be attacked.

"In most women who suffer recurrent miscarriages, the father's tissue type is so similar to his wife's tissue type, this 'tolerance' signal is not sent to the mother-to-be. Without the signal, the mother fails to produce a normal 'blocking' message that tells her immune system not to attack the fetus. No protective blocking antibodies are produced. Her immune system attacks the fetus as though it were an enemy.

"By 'immunizing' a woman with a specific protein from her husband's sperm, we can trick her immune system into producing the very critical blocking antibodies that will later stop her immune system from attacking her fetus. This immunization approach will help eighty-eight percent of women who have lost three or more pregnancies to become pregnant."

I sent copies of the studies to the woman, telling her to show the studies to her doctor in France. Over a year later, I received a picture of the woman, her husband, and their newborn daughter.

This woman had to go beyond positive thinking in order to have her baby. Positivity was the groundwork, action was the instrument. It's true that it was easier for me, a physician, to find the right action in this case. I knew whom to call. But she could have done it herself. It may have taken more phone calls and letters, but sooner or later she would have come across the studies that helped her have a baby.

Positive thinking is important; it's absolutely necessary. Without a positive outlook, we won't try. The French woman stopped looking because she lost her positivity. But if we don't act we won't see progress, and our positive belief will soon fade. Positive thinking, positive action.

ACTION 9,000 TIMES OVER

"Do what you can, with what you have, where you are."
                                                    -Theodore Roosevelt

Action can accomplish miracles. In the summer of 1989, I found myself sitting in a large convention hall in Dallas, Texas, listening to a young man teach us about action and courage. His name was W. Mitchel. Some years ago, he had been taking flying lessons. One day, while riding his motorcycle home from the airport, he was hit by a truck. Mitchel was pinned beneath his fallen bike, but he wasn't badly hurt. He thought everything would be OK when suddenly the bike burst into flames, burning Mitchel over much of his body. Luckily, a passing motorist slammed on the brakes, grabbed a fire extinguisher out of his trunk and doused the flames before they killed Mitchel. The emergency crews arrived, and Mitchel was rushed to the hospital.

Burn pain is horrible pain. I've seen many burned patients writhing in agony in their hospital beds, screaming for morphine, crying for relief, begging for death. I remember one horrible burned man I saw when I was still a student. He was— I don't know how else to describe him—charred black, skin and muscle were burned away. Simultaneously fascinated and repulsed, I slowly reached out to his little toe, touching it as gently as I could. As I touched the toe it fell off and turned to ash, right in front of my horrified eyes.

Mitchel told us that he recovered, as well as anyone can recover from being so badly burned. The scars never completely healed, and he had lost some of his fingers, but things were looking up. He learned to accept the disfiguring scars, to overlook the stares. Business was booming, his social life was good. He resumed flying lessons, earning various licenses and advanced ratings.

One day, while taking some friends up in his plane for a spin, something went terribly wrong. They had barely gotten off the runway, only seventy-five feet into the air, when disaster struck. The plane fell from the sky like a rock. When the plane hit the ground, Mitchel, worried about fire, shouted to his passengers: "Get out, get out!" They quickly scrambled out to safety; then it was Mitchel's turn. He started to move but nothing happened. He couldn't figure out why; he thought he had to try harder. He kept trying to get out, harder and harder, but his body would not respond. He couldn't understand why he couldn't get himself out of the wreckage; he wasn't pinned in. Then it dawned on him. He was paralyzed. No amount of trying was going to get his legs to move.

In the days and weeks that followed, he asked himself over and over: "Why me? What did I do to deserve this?" Through all the tests, through the doctors and the therapies he wondered, "Why me?"

And now in the summer of 1989, he sat before us in his wheelchair, on stage, speaking to a packed house. We saw and we heard a strong man, a man who wouldn't let anything stop him. We held our breath when he said: "I used to be able to do ten thousand things." We stood and cheered when he thundered: "Now I can only do *nine* thousand!" He said it with a grin—he said it proudly, for he was telling us that he was living life to its fullest—he was full of action, wheelchair or no wheelchair. "If I do even a fraction of the nine thousand things I'm capable of doing, then I'm living life to the hilt."

Burned, missing some fingers, paralyzed and confined to a wheelchair, Mitchel is still a man of action. How many of us can do nine thousand things? With two good legs, without having been burned, how many of us do nine thousand things? How many things do we do? How much action are we capable of? Ten things, twenty, fifty, one hundred things? That's the limit we unknowingly place on our lives. Many of us can't even *think* of nine thousand things, let alone *do* them. Mitchel didn't worry about what he couldn't do. His eyes were set on what he *could* do. Mitchel could see nine thousand great things to do. And what about the other thousand, the things he couldn't do anymore? He didn't waste a thought on them.

If anyone had an excuse to lock himself up in a dark room and curse the world, it was Mitchel. But he was a positive

thinker. He believed that things would get better. He
believed that he could recover—that he *would* recover. And
Mitchel did recover, because he took action. He underwent
medical treatment, he continued his flying lessons, he went
back to work.

Positive thinking was essential to Mitchel's recovery—but it
was only half the equation. Positive thoughts *plus* positive
action.

POSITIVE THOUGHTS, POSITIVE ACTION:
THE PTPA PERSON

"If you ever need a helping hand,
you'll find one at the end of your arm."
                                  -Yiddish Proverb

In my thirty-plus years of practicing Internal Medicine and
Cardiology, I've seen numerous people use their positive
thoughts to beat their diseases and turn their lives around. As
Barry and I travel around the country, people tell us that positive thinking is a medicine. But many others tell us that it's not
enough. They say that they have tried to think positively, that
they have recited positive affirmations every day, but could not
shake off their negativity, doubt, anger, fear and frustration.
They knew that their thoughts were an important key to their
health, but they just couldn't *turn* that key.

"Give me more," we'd be asked. "I want to do nine thousand things. Hey, I'll settle for five thousand things. Give me
another way, give me something extra."

For many very good people, like the French woman who
yearned for a child, positive thinking was not enough. The
"something extra" that so many of us need is action.

Creating Facts

Those of us who find that positive thinking isn't enough must add action to the equation. Positive thoughts, positive action. Searching for the answer is a positive action. Forgiving someone is a positive action. Applying for a new job, developing a new skill, asking the right questions, going someplace; these can all be positive actions. Wishing we had the answer, knowing that the answer is out there, is a great start. Now we must go look for the answer.

We act in order to "create facts." The fact that we can not have a baby is unacceptable. We take action to create a new fact. The answer is not always available, and it may not be the answer we want. But if we don't act, we won't find the right answers that are usually out there. Years ago my wife, Hannah, and I were hit with the sad fact that our third child would spend his life as near to blind as one could be. All the authorities told us that it was a fact. I was still in medical training. I believed them. Hannah didn't. She believed that Steven would be able to see, someday, somehow. She believed it. Period. Each of the many "nos" she received from doctors great and small brought her closer to the "yes" that gave our son sight. Positive thoughts plus positive action finally lead her to a doctor with a new idea. Thirty years later, as I write this, Steven and his partner are hurrying to arrange the furniture in their brand new law offices, Laing and Fox. Why the rush? Steve's got to get going, he's playing racquetball this evening.

We're All Believers

"That's a great story," some say when I tell them about my wife's search for my son's sight. "But she was already a positive thinker. It's easy to act if you already have faith, but I don't."

Everyone has faith. Most of us have tremendous faith. Unfortunately, many of us have negative faith. We *know* it's not going to work out, we *know* we don't measure up, we *know* we're going to fail. We're believers. We believe in the wrong things. Many of the bad things we bring upon ourselves could be turned to good if we focused the tremendous power of our faith in a different direction.

Mitchel, the pilot, had tremendous faith and he jumped into action. But what if we have negative faith, what if we find it difficult to act? Can we change our faith? Can we break an addiction to negativity? You bet we can! With action. But sometimes a different kind of action is required.

Light Always Shines in the Darkness

I learned about faith and action—a very unusual kind of action, from a small, frail-looking woman I met many years ago, when I had barely completed my medical training. Sally, a survivor of the Nazi concentration camps, lay amongst perhaps twenty other women in a large hospital ward, dying of cancer. Her skin was waxen, her short hair lay flat and lifeless on her head, but it was obvious that she had once been a beautiful woman.

Sally was considered a very troublesome patient, especially back then, when people were supposed to quietly submit to whatever treatment (or lack of treatment) we doctors deemed appropriate. Sally was "uncooperative." She demanded to know what was in each syringe before she would let the nurse give her a shot; she insisted on a justification for each test before she would allow it to be performed; she had to know what each medicine was supposed to do. She complained about the food, the stuffy air in the ward, the uncomfortable bed. And oddly enough, she absolutely insisted upon keeping a lit candle on her nightstand. Every time I went by her bed, a candle was burning. I assumed she had it there for religious comfort.

The physicians, nurses and technicians soon learned it was easier to go along with her demands than argue it out. Besides, everyone "knew" she was going to die soon. I noticed that one of the senior doctors had written "SDTH" on her chart. "SDTH" meant "start digging the hole." It was his way of telling the other doctors that there was no hope.

Late one night, when most everyone had gone home, when a lone nurse or two watched over all twenty women, and when snores mingled with troubled coughs and moans and sobs, I sat by Sally's bed, listening to her tales of the concentration camps. "I was a political prisoner," she told me, "a foolish little girl caught with my friends before we did anything, that's how incompetent we were."

After she described some of her adventures, I asked her how she had survived the camps, trying to imagine the young girl dragged off a train or a truck and thrown into a hell hole. I asked her how anyone survived the starvation, the savage beatings, the abusive overwork, the exposure to winter's snow, protected by only a few rags.

Sally told me that the ones who survived were the ones who believed they would survive. Today we would say they were the positive thinkers. The ones who didn't believe, she explained, quickly died. The believers constantly looked, bargained and schemed for an extra scrap of bread, a little piece of cloth or paper to help keep themselves warm, a better bunk, a tiny sliver of soap with which to wash themselves. The believers grabbed every little something extra.

Those who did not believe they could survive had a look in their eyes, she explained. You could tell they had faith—negative faith. They *knew* they were going to die. They never looked for that extra crumb to eat, that bit of paper to stuff into an ill-fitting shoe that was rubbing their foot raw and bloody. Those who did not look, of course, never saw their opportunities. Even in a concentration camp, there were some—granted, very few—but *some* opportunities.

"Then you must have believed you would make it right from the start," I said, marveling at the strength of the young Sally.

Her answer startled me: "No. I thought I would be dead in a week. Some of the other women tried to teach me how to survive, but I knew I was going to die. I didn't try."

"If you didn't try, how did you stay alive?"

In her roundabout way (so frustrating to a young man who wanted answers now!), Sally told how her faith turned from negative to positive. An older woman, a veteran prisoner, made Sally join her in a little ritual she performed every morning and evening. Snatching back from the Nazis a few seconds of time twice a day, the woman lit an imaginary candle with an imaginary match. Setting the imaginary candle into a non-existent holder, she stepped back, admiring the flame that was not there. Surrounded by filthy, starving, disease-ridden women who most likely would not survive the change of seasons, the stench of death always in the air, she completed the ritual by whispering, "Light always shines in the darkness."

That skeleton of a woman, weakened by who knew how many years in the camp, forced Sally to "light" her own candle every chance she got. The woman and the girl usually "lit" their candles entirely in their minds, while standing in ranks waiting to be counted, while marching to and from work, while in their bunks at night.

"The funny thing was," Sally told me, "somehow that nonsense made me believe I could survive. You're a doctor— you know better, but I think that what we do can change what we think. Even if we don't believe it in the beginning. That's

why I keep the candle with me now. Lighting a real candle is
even better than the mental candle. So I light it every day and
say 'Light always shines in the darkness.' That's how I'm going
to outlive this cancer."

Frankly, I thought she was a little nutty. Fresh from my
Residency in Internal Medicine, I knew all about the latest
drugs and procedures. I knew, for a fact, that lighting imaginary candles would not alter body chemistry one bit. A few
minutes later I was called away to an emergency in another
part of the hospital. Caught up in the swirl of patients and
consultations and running from hospital to hospital, I forgot
about Sally and her candle. A few days later I noticed that
somebody else was in Sally's bed. I made a mental note to ask
the nurse what had happened to that tough woman and her
candles, but forgot to inquire. I never did find out what
happened to her.

I was too busy to remember back then; then when I did not
understand how a girl could be saved by a candle that existed
nowhere but in her mind. Years later, when people would ask
how they could act if they did not believe, I would remember
Sally and her imaginary candle. I also thought about the real
candle she fought to keep at her bedside. Lighting a candle
was an action. But instead of changing the outside world, this
action was designed to change Sally's internal world—the
world of her thoughts. In the beginning, she couldn't act
because she didn't believe. So she acted to create belief, then
took action to survive.

Light always shines in the darkness. The light of our
action can shine in the darkness of our disbelief.

Two Types of Action

Mitchel, the pilot, was full of action. He could do nine

thousand things. His action was directed outward, it was specifically goal-oriented. He had physical therapy after the accidents, he went back to work, he continued his flying lessons. He had positive thoughts, and he took positive action.

Then there are other kinds of actions, equally powerful, but different in content and intent. Lighting an imaginary candle, striking a tiny flame powerful enough to light the darkness of a death camp, is a powerful action. But it's a symbolic, inner-directed action. Rather than change something in the "real" world, this kind of action seeks to change our "inner" world.

Mitchel's action is outward, Sally's is inward. Mitchel acts because he believes. Sally acted in order to believe. Through the years, people like Sally have devised their own symbolic, very personal, inner-directed actions designed to bring their positive thoughts to life.

Every morning a woman with terminal cancer, a woman whom we doctors had given up on, picked up a beautiful wine goblet. On the goblet were inscribed the words: "My Cup Runneth Over." Lying in her hospital bed, she literally filled her goblet with water, allowing the water to run over onto her hand. She didn't simply tell herself that her cup runneth over, she saw it and felt it. She went beyond belief to make her thoughts tangible. We doctors told her to go home and die. She insisted upon having surgery, which itself could have killed her, and lived. She beat her cancer—the cancer we doctors pronounced incurable. Like Sally, that bedridden woman with cancer used this symbolic, inwardly-directed action to create the belief that she could survive.

"Inward" action is like painting a picture, a picture of what we would like to occur. "Inward" action is designed to conjure up the conditions, and the belief that makes other action possible. "Inward" action is a command to believe, a command that can be written, as if in stone, upon our subconscious.

I remember a developmentally handicapped young woman who kept a shoebox filled with small, polished stones in her bedroom. Every day she'd reach into the box to grab two big handfuls of stones, each little stone representing something she could do. Never accepting the limited life so many people insisted she was condemned to, she grasped new handfuls of "possibilities" every day to remind herself that life was as big as her beliefs. Yes, she had been born with limits, but everyday she grabbed onto new handfuls of possibility, and everyday she took another figurative step forward.

Lighting a candle or filling a cup to overflowing will not, by itself, strengthen your immune system any more than holding onto a bunch of polished rocks makes us any smarter. These actions are symbols—no, they're more than symbols; they are concrete representations of thoughts, they're projections, images of the mind made real. They are pictures of thought; living, moving, breathing, three-dimensional pictures of our ephemeral inner world. The woman who overcame her cancer told me that her action (filling her goblet until it overflowed) not only mirrored, it strengthened her belief. Sometimes, she said, the act created new layers of belief. "After the fifth doctor told me, in essence, to go home and die," she explained, "it was a little hard to think wonderful thoughts. So I acted. I picked up my goblet and let it overflow. I watched it overflow. I felt it overflow into my hand for a long time. Finally, I began to think about living again."

"Inward" actions deal with the possible, the desired, the future. It helps create the very belief that makes action possible. You fill your cup to overflowing after you've been told that cancer has dried your cup of life because you need to create the belief. You light a candle in the darkness because you can't see the possibilities for survival.

Some people scoff at the "inward" action. They say it's silly, it's airy-fairy 1960-ish nonsense. How can lighting a candle or pouring water into a glass compare with an antibiotic or surgery? As you'll see, action, both inward and outward, compares quite well with the traditional tools of medicine. Quite well indeed. Our physical lives are largely dependent upon what happens in our minds. Every picture painted by a thought directly affects our bodies.

This is a book about doing. We'll examine and prescribe all types of action. You'll discover how to learn to believe in yourself, and how to use that belief to make yourself healthier, smarter, more successful, even sexier. The key is to go beyond belief: *Positive Thoughts, Positive Action* (PTPA).

They say that a picture is worth a thousand words. We say that an action creates a thousand thoughts. And even if an action creates but one thought, if it is the right one, it can turn your life around.

R_x: ACTION!

"The only limit to our realization of tomorrow
will be our doubts of today."
-Franklin Delano Roosevelt

Our prescription for health, happiness and success begins with action. Good nutrition, good medical care and many other things are also necessary, but it begins with action! The man who could do 9,000 things had every reason to pull the covers over his head and die. Instead he took action—physical, mental and emotional action. Whether it was by himself or with the help of others, he acted! The young girl thrown into a concentration camp "knew" that she was going to die. Someone else forced her to act as if she would live. At first she didn't believe it. She lit the imaginary candle because she had to, but in time, simply doing the action changed her belief.

We're going to give you tools for helping to create belief, then to go beyond belief with action. By the time you finish this book, you'll have a list of specific outward things to do, such as mending a quarrel, searching out a forgotten friend, making up a new resume, and so on. You'll also have a series of inward actions to make a part of your everyday life, such as filling your cup to over-flowing and feeling, literally feeling, the water as it flows over.

Lighting the Darkness

Light always shines in the darkness. A tiny flicker of belief can burn away the darkness of fear. Let's light the darkness. At night, in the early morning, or during the day with the blinds drawn, light a candle. A simple little candle will do. In the darkness, looking down at your candle, hold your hands above the candle, palms up, one resting on the other. (Hold them high enough above the flame so that they are not burned.) Notice that your palms are dark. Now separate your hands, turn them so that your thumbs are on top. Cup your hands and lower them down to the flame. Hold your hands to the sides of the flame, close enough to feel a little bit of warmth (but not too close). Notice that the palms of your hands, facing the flame, are lit. It's as if you hold the light of belief in your hands. Look into your handful of light as you say:

What are my limits, where are my boundaries,
Where is the edge of my universe?
The edge is at the end of the light,
The light I hold in my hand.

How far can I see, how much can I know,
How deep is my understanding?
Dark mysteries come clear in the light,
The light I hold in my hand.

How deep dare I go, how much can I bear,
Is another step one step too far?
Icy burdens melt in the light,
The light I hold in my hand.

As I spread my hands my world opens wide,
My world is as great as my reach.
I open my hands, open my world,
Open to love, action and joy.

What are my limits, how much can I know,
Is another step one step too far?
There are no limits, no boundaries, no end,
If the light I hold in my hand.

Does lighting a candle seem a little silly? Some think so. Sally thought that lighting an imaginary candle was absolute nonsense—*but it worked*! "Inward" action creates belief, and with belief, many things are possible.

P.S. On Being a Hero

Many of our great heroes have been men and women of action. So have some of our smallest heroes. I met a hero, a real live hero named Mark, years ago, when I coached the Little League Dodgers at Roxbury Park in Beverly Hills. Mark was a broad-shouldered eight year old with a big smile, dark curly hair and cerebral palsy. Cerebral palsy is a descriptive term we doctors apply to a variety of motor disorders of the body which result from brain damage during gestation. Although the victims have normal intelligence, their cerebral palsy produces a kind of spastic paralysis of various parts of the body, trembling and other problems.

The other kids used to laugh when they saw him swing a bat or throw a ball. The other boys were developing smooth, fluid motions, but Mark's arms and hands shook all the time. They'd laugh when he ran to first base, looking like a cross between the Tin Man and a drunk. They called him "Spaaaaz"—that's how they said it, "Spaaaaz," holding out the "a." But from the moment I met him, I felt drawn to this little boy with a big smile who kept jumping up and down and telling me that he was gong to win a trophy.

The season was exciting and successful for we Dodgers— except Mark. He wanted to get a hit so badly, but he never got close. He couldn't catch a ball if you put it into his mitt. Everyone kept telling Mark that he was a loser. When he came up to bat the other team would scream "SPAAAAZ! SPAAAAZ!" But Mark believed in himself, and he constantly acted on that great belief. He acted by coming to every practice and game early, a glove on one shaky hand, a ball in the other, always eager, always excited. He never stopped practicing—catching, throwing, hitting, running. He bore the inevitable disappointments, the taunts and the insults, remarkably well. Occasionally his big smile was melted off— was burned off—by the cruelty of the other boys. I wouldn't allow my boys to make fun of him, but I couldn't control the other kids. Or the parents sitting in the stands. They were perhaps cruelest of all.

Once, and only once, Mark ran off the field in tears, the jeers from the other boys ringing in his the ears. When I caught up with him he told me that he wanted so much to hit a home run, to be a great ballplayer. Once, just once in his life, he wanted to be the hero. I told Mark that he already was a hero. Anyone lucky enough to have been born with talent can hit a home run. It takes something special to strike out a thousand times, and keep smiling.

The little boy stopped shaking. He wiped away the tears as he gave me a grateful smile, then turned and ran back onto the field.

We came to the last game of the season. A win would get us into the play-offs. Mark came up to bat with the bases loaded—and struck out. An easy ground ball was hit to him in right field—he missed it. The other boys begged me to bench the "Spaaaaz." The parents in the stands demanded I do so: "This is an important game," they said, "This is for the play-offs. Bench that Spaaaaz!"

They were right. I had already let Mark play a couple of innings, and he had had a chance to bat and a chance to field. And this was an important game. Any reasonable coach would have taken Mark out of the game at that point. But he had practiced more and had practiced harder than any other kid in the league. He kept his head high when others tried to tear him down. He didn't give up. I left Mark in.

He struck out twice more and made more errors. He was costing us the game—our shot at the play-offs. Last inning, the bases were loaded, two outs. We needed a run to stay alive, two runs to win. Mark stepped up to the plate as they shouted "Spaaaaz," and "Shake it up, baby."

His arms and legs trembled as he waited for the pitch. He swung a mighty swing, a swing that would send the ball sailing over the fence. The ball dribbled down the third base line, barely moving. We were stunned; he had actually hit the ball. In retrospect, I don't think he hit the ball. I think the ball hit his bat. We all stood there, staring at the ball. Mark lurched toward first base, arms and legs flailing. The pitcher and third baseman finally moved for the ball, charged for the ball. It was like one of these movies, where everything is in slow motion. Mark running for first base, the pitcher snatching up the ball, wheeling, throwing...

Mark was safe at first! He got his hit, he knocked in two runs, he won the game. The other Dodgers poured out of the dugout, they slapped him on the back, and hugged him. Mark jumped up and down, he shouted for joy, tears ran down his face. If anyone had been looking at me, they would have seen me crying with him.

Ralph Waldo Emerson said that a hero is someone who hangs on for five minutes more. And what are they doing while they're hanging on? They're taking action! Even if their action is nothing more than refusing to quit, they're taking action. Mark was a great hero. He hung on for a life-time.

Where have all our heroes gone? They're out there. You just have to know where to look. I believe that we could all be heroes, if we believe in ourselves, and if we act on that belief. Hold the light in your hand.

CHAPTER TWO

THE PATCHWORK PARABLE

*"Life affords no higher pleasure than
that of surmounting difficulties..."*
—Samuel Johnson

As a 6-year old boy, I roamed the streets of South Philly wearing a faded yellow corduroy jacket. I was proud of that jacket. It had a zipper in the front, and elastic on the cuffs—a big deal for 1934. There were three buttons on each sleeve, right above the cuffs. In my mind, those faded buttons weren't hanging by a thread on the cuffs. And they weren't battered wooden discs, they were bright shiny stars—the stars of a major-general. When I put on that jacket, I wasn't a poor kid living in unheated boarding rooms—I was the Commander in Chief! Often times, in the freezing weather, I lined up some of the younger kids in the neighborhood and marched them through the snow, up and down South Reese Street. The older boys snickered as I paraded by with my little army, snapping to attention and giving me mock salutes.

I was proud of that yellow corduroy jacket—yet I was a little ashamed of it, as well. I hoped that no one knew the "secret" of my jacket. You see, we lived in South Philly, the poorest part of Philadelphia, through the Depression. Most of my friends were from families we would now call the "working poor." Their fathers had some type of work—a butcher, a breadmaker, a truck or taxi driver. Their parents made barely enough to pay the rent on a little row house, even though rent was only $10 or so. There were no floor coverings in their homes, except, in the occasional house, linoleum, that cold plastic-like substance which usually had some garish design printed on it. Sheets served as window shades. Norman was the "richest" of my friends. His father was a plumber, and their house had real window shades, rugs, and a tiny little porch. I thought that was really living.

They were the working poor, while I was of the "sometimes working" poor. I'd blush whenever anyone mentioned my yellow corduroy jacket. Did they know the secret? They must have known that my mother couldn't have bought it for me as we didn't have the money for a jacket that nice. They certainly knew that my father, intelligent and strong as he was, was usually "between jobs." Oh, he was bright and he had a strong back, he could quote chapter and verse from the Bible and he was full of folk wisdom. But he could never tear those demons from his soul. He literally fought with his bosses and other men. All his natural wisdom couldn't stop him from drowning in anger, that terrible rage he could not articulate, in alcohol.

Like many other children, I was born with the cards stacked against me. My father, a fruit broker, did not often hold a steady job, and never for very long. His drinking and fighting cost us dearly. At least once, he fled town, hiding out in Baltimore from the mobster whose jaw he'd broken in a poker game. My mother was a maid at the Germantown Boy's Home, half her meager salary going to pay for the woman who took care of me. Later, she sewed buttons on shirts. If she went to the bathroom, the boss yelled at her for slowing down the line. For years, we lived in a succession of rented rooms, sometimes with relatives, sometimes with heat, sometimes without.

Everyday, it was drummed into my young head that I was headed nowhere. Even at school, I remember so well the teacher who would say to us, his right hand slowly chopping into his left palm: "You boys should quit school and become garbage collectors." When I said I wanted to be a doctor, they laughed and told me to stop dreaming. They told me I was a foolish kid, that I didn't know how bad things were. They described, in great detail, all the obstacles waiting to trip me up. I was the poorest boy in my little corner of South Philly, in the midst of the Depression. I was regularly suspended from school. I threw a brick through a police car window on a dare. My father drank to hide from his anger, my mother pushed a broom and made beds. It was pretty clear to everyone that I was headed nowhere fast.

Everyday I was told that life was lousy. Everyday I knew my parents struggled to put food on my plate. Everyday I knew my father drank too much. Every winter day, I didn't know if we'd have any heat. Intellectually, deep down, I knew things were grim. But I refused to accept "reality." "I'd put on my yellow corduroy jacket and become "General Arnie." I'd put on my yellow corduroy jacket and "reality" would melt away. There was no Depression, we weren't poor, my father didn't drink. Instead, our mansion was filled with food, heat and good cheer: I was "General Arnie," head-chief-top general of the whole Army.

I often wanted to give everyone else yellow corduroy jackets so they, too, could become generals or ballerinas or Rockerfellers or Einsteins or whatever they wanted to be. I wondered why they so stubbornly preferred harsh reality to beautiful dreams. But I was only a child.

A Reason to Dream

I loved that yellow corduroy jacket, worn and beaten as it was. I was also a bit ashamed of the jacket; I'd blush when they asked where I got such a nice one. I remember walking miles with my mother one day, past the city dump to the railroad tracks. On that particular day someone stood inside a railroad car, tossing used clothing out to the crowd of poor people. Shamefaced, my mother pulled me through the crowd, to near the front. All of the sudden she leapt up and grabbed that yellow corduroy jacket as it sailed from the railroad car. She leapt and snatched it like an outfielder shagging a fly ball against the left field wall in the World Series. Then she tucked it under her arm and, towing me behind, pushed her way through the crowd like a halfback plowing through the defensive line on the way to a touchdown.

Maybe I loved that jacket so much because it made one of my dreams come true; I became a general when I wore it. No, I take that back. The jacket didn't *make* my dream come true, rather, it gave me something else to dream about.

I dreamt a lot as a kid. With my yellow jacket on, I was a general. With a little bottle in my hand, I was a great doctor, discovering the cure for tuberculosis. When I walked down 7th Street, amidst all those pushcarts, I was a rich man bellying up to the buffet, not a hungry kid without a penny in my pocket. The older boys taught me how to turn my dreams into a full stomach. No money? No problem. I'd walk by a push cart loaded with fruit and, as quickly as I later learned to cut a suture, I'd grab an apple and shove it into my partially-opened yellow corduroy jacket.

My friends and I used to stand outside Glider's Restaurant. Noses to the glass, we'd watch the "rich" people sitting at tables, being served steaks, stuffed cabbage, noodle soup. Some of my friends were angry because they couldn't eat at Gliders, or any other restaurant. They resented the people they watched so enviously. I couldn't go in there either, but I didn't resent anyone. I dreamt that someday I'd walk right in and join them. I *knew* I would. I could see it in my dream.

Maybe that was why I was happy, why things didn't get me

down. I didn't resent others who had more. I simply dreamt
of the day when I would also have. Why be angry when you
can joyfully look forward to plenty?

Most of all, I dreamt of being a doctor—a great doctor like
Dr. Cooper. Dr. Cooper was our family doctor, an old-fash-
ioned physician who walked up and down the streets making
house calls, who accepted food or chickens or whatever else
the patient had in lieu of a fee, who often took nothing at all,
if the patient had nothing to give. (Barry, my son and co-
author, is named after that great man.)

Ten Thousand Reasons to be "Realistic"

It seemed that most everyone told me to be realistic, to
stop dreaming. They'd say:

- *You be a doctor? Don't be ridiculous.*
- *You're banging your head against a stone wall.*
- *People like us haven't got a chance.*
- *Don't make me laugh.*
- *There's no way a poor boy like you can do that.*
- *What good is life? We suffer and we die. Everyone is out
  to get you.*
- *The world won't be here much longer, anyhow.*
- *You're going to fail.*
- *Life is stacked against people like us.*
- *You haven't got enough money.*
- *You're bound to get sick.*
- *Don't ever turn your back on them.*
- *You don't know the right people. You've got to know the
  right people.*
- *You'll wind up like your father.*

And on and on and on. They had ten thousand reasons to be absolutely "realistic." Unfortunately, to be so definitely—and defiantly—realistic meant to be unhappy. These were nice people, those who insisted I firmly ground myself in unhappy "reality." They were good, hard-working, well-meaning, very realistic people. They "knew" that poor boys from the wrong side of the tracks did not become generals or doctors. They "knew" that dreaming was a waste of time when there was work to do. They "knew" that dreaming was bound to lead to disappointment. Why get your hopes up, they would say. The higher your hopes, the harder you'll fall.

A few people encouraged my dreaming. A few people told me to stop looking at the garbage all around me and start reaching for the stars. Not all the star-gazers make it, they explained, but only the star-gazers have a chance. And if you've got a chance, they said, you've got everything you need.

My parents, poor as they were, always encouraged my "crazy dreams." When I told them I wanted to be a doctor, they thought it was a great idea. Everyone else told me I was crazy. No one from this neighborhood ever goes to college, let alone medical school. No one in this neighborhood has the brains, the money, the connections, the what-have-you. But Mom and Dad said I was going to be a great doctor. Dad had three years of schooling before he had to work to help support the family. Mom left the farm school after tenth grade. College and medical school were beyond their horizons. They had nothing to give me but hope. And that, I found, turned out to be the best thing they could possibly give me.

There are ten thousand reasons to be absolutely "realistic" and to absolutely "know" that your life is miserable. There's only one reason to dream: You can't grab onto a star unless you reach for it.

What Are Dreams?

When you dream, I was told growing up, you're hiding from reality. The only way to survive, they would say, is to face harsh reality, head on. Don't reach out with your dreams. Pull in, get your guard up, protect yourself. What they said made sense—to them.

I'm a physician, trained in the rigors and exactitudes of science. Dreaming is non-scientific. Dreams are for the psychiatrists, we young medical students were told. Your job is to master the reality of the human body, of germs and medicines.

What is dreaming? What is reality? Reality is what we know to be true, what we can analyze, verify and quantify, what we can touch, if not with our hands, then with our high-tech tools. But dreams, they say, dreams are but footprints left by wandering thoughts, they are shadows twice-removed. Yet, dreams, these footprints of the night, often come true. I am a physician, just as I had envisioned. I can afford to eat at Gliders Restaurant (if it's still there), or fashionable Jimmy's or the Bistro here in Beverly Hills, every night of the week. Were my dreams mental fluff, or were they an early glimpse of later reality?

Having lived on both the top and bottom of the heap, I can tell you that our dreams *are* reality—they are very real projections of what we want to be. Dreams are mirrors to our mind, blueprints for our future. Yes, many of our dreams are exaggerated, outrageous, but they speak for our silent soul. Our dreams are that part of us which tells us that we can be something great, something exciting, something exotic, something wonderful. Our dreams are our soul's request that we keep moving, growing, learning, loving, giving, tasting, smelling, daring, even failing, and that we just keep trying. Dreaming is our soul's way of spurring us on, of giving us reason to look for and to reach for the stars. And dreams *are* reality. Dreams create reality: The reality of now, and the reality we hope will be.

Double-Edged Reality

Most people will agree that dreams are "real" in that they tell us what we want to be, but they are not "present reality." A dream may encourage us to go to college to become what we want to be, but how can a dream change the "reality" of right now? That's impossible. Or is it?

At any time, for every situation, there are two "realities." One reality consists of the facts: It's two-twenty on the afternoon of January 19th. I'm sitting at my desk as Barry and I write these words. I'm sitting on a black chair; he's sitting on the couch. I'm wearing a blue shirt with white stripes. I just finished speaking on the phone with an old friend. We're only eight pages into this new section. Will we have enough to make a whole chapter?

That's the hard fact reality. Here's the other reality: I'm excited about what we're writing. This is great information! I get teary-eyed remembering my yellow corduroy jacket. I get a lump in my throat thinking about my parents. With all their faults, they did all they knew how to for me. They *always* encouraged me to be great. That phone call from my friend was a pain in the neck because it interrupted my train of thoughts and memories.

Two realities: The *facts* and the *interpretation*. We can't always control the facts, but we can determine our interpretation.

The Patchwork Uniform

I was still a very poor boy when I joined the Boy Scouts. Of course, I wanted a uniform—a shiny new uniform with leggings and blouse, with hat and scarf, with a chest full of badges to wear proudly to meetings, to school, and on the street. But uniforms cost money, more money than I had. I had worked ever since I was seven. My first job was selling chewing gum in the park. But I gave all my earnings to my mother, to help with the rent. There was no money to pay for a uniform. (Years later, when I began college, she gave me what seemed like a huge sum of money to me. It turned out that she had saved every penny I gave her, put it in her piggy bank for my college education.)

The other boys, poor as their families were, got their uniforms. I felt like the lowest of the low when I went to the meetings in my regular clothes. Then I managed to put together 50¢ to buy an official Boy Scout neckerchief. Soon I had two more nickels, enough to get the little slide that held the neckerchief in place around my neck.

Was I proud of my "uniform!" The factual "reality" was that I did not have a real uniform. But my interpretation was that I had a wonderful uniform. Other boys laughed at me, but in my dreamer's mind, I was dressed to the Boy Scout hilt! I'd go on outings with my kerchief around my neck, and I'd wear it to school on the designated days. Later I got a used shirt, a few sizes too large, and some ill-fitting pants someone else had discarded. The pants had been washed a thousand times. They were worn and bleached out. Oh, they used to laugh at my patchwork uniform, they would call me the "King of the Rags." The factual reality was that I was wearing castoffs— torn, worn, leftovers. In my mind, however, it was the best, shiniest, most wonderful uniform a boy could have.

According to the factual reality, I should have been unhappy. I should have taken my poverty to heart. I should have burned with shame when they laughed at my patchwork uniform. By all factual reality, I should have spent my childhood railing at my awful fate. I should have been miserable (as many of my friends were).

But thanks to my interpretative reality, my dream reality, I was deliriously happy. With just a kerchief and a slide, I was the best Boy Scout there ever was. Wearing my yellow corduroy jacket, I was general of the Army.

"So what," many people have said to Barry and me, "So you were fooling yourself into thinking you were happy. Big deal."

It was a big deal, probably the biggest, best deal of my life. I can't tell you how many of my friends, how many of their parents, how many of all the poor, down-trodden people in South Philly and everywhere else lived lives of misery because they focused on the factual reality. If you tell yourself, for a lifetime, that you are miserable and unhappy, that you are nothing and will go nowhere, you are absolutely right. But if you tell yourself, just once in a while, that you are happy and that you can reach the stars, you're also right.

My parents left me no money. Their legacy to me was greater than gold: They made me believe that all my handicaps were nothing more than paper chains, waiting to be broken. When I said I was a General, they told me I was *the* General. When I said I was going to be a doctor, they said I was going to be the best doctor there ever was. When I said I was going to get out of the ghetto, they smiled and said, "and so it is written."

A Patchwork Future

A few years ago, I sat in the sun-lit stands on a Sunday afternoon, watching as my granddaughter Melanie "graduated" from the Girl Scout Daisys into the Brownies. Melanie's mother Robin, their scout leader, took each girl's Daisy sash off, replacing it with a Brownie sash. The little girls were very excited as they recited their pledges and sang some songs.

Immediately after the ceremony, Melanie and many of her

friends put their Daisy sashes into a box. The sashes were going to be donated to poor girls who couldn't afford sashes. The sashes were a little worn out; they had a few stains, a little rip here and there, but they were official Daisy sashes. Somewhere, some underprivileged girls opened that box of used sashes. I imagine that some of the girls, steeped in factual reality, turned up their noses and refused to wear castoffs from the rich kids. Some of the girls, steeped in factual reality, were probably angry because they had to accept charity. But I hope that at least one of the girls was so happy to have a sash—even if it didn't fit, even if it was stained or a bit torn. I hope that at least one girl would be so proud of her Daisy sash!

Who's better off? The ones who match the grim face of factual reality with their own frowning faces, or the one who pretends that her patchwork uniform is a gown fit for a Daisy princess?

"He's the poorest of the poor, and the happiest of the happy." That's what I heard some of my friends parent's say of me in whispered wonderment when I was little. Why is he so happy when he lives so miserably? they wondered. And there were plenty of lows in those years. But with my yellow corduroy jacket, my patchwork uniform and my dreams, how could I help but smile?

I was happy because my parents taught me to change "reality" by interpreting it as good. My interpretation couldn't fill my often-empty belly or buy me a new uniform. My interpretation could always, however, help me keep my chin up and my eyes twinkling at the stars.

A Dream—and a Push

I don't mean, of course, that if we're starving, we can simply dream that our stomachs are full. I certainly don't advocate dreaming about being safe when a car is careening your way—I'd say face reality and jump out of the way, right now! I simply mean to say that dreams are paint brushes in our hands, inviting us to color the canvas of our lives. Our canvas is not completely blank, some lines and colors are already there and we can't change them. But otherwise we are the artist, the Da Vinci, the Picasso who paints the picture of our lives, exactly as we see fit.

Life did not see fit to draw a beautiful Boy Scout uniform into the picture of my life. Still, why stare gloomily at a bare picture, when you can paint the costume in yourself, with your dreams? And when you do, you absolutely alter reality. Not the factual reality of your uniform; an old piece of cloth is an old piece of cloth. Rather, you change the interpretative reality of yourself, of your emotions, and, through your emotions, your biochemistry, and your entire being. Why agree with the factual reality that says I'm unhappy because people are laughing at my patchwork uniform, when I can embrace the reality that has me jumping for joy?

First Aid Merit Badge:
Stepping Stone to Medical School

One day, when I was twelve years old, I proudly wore my patchwork uniform to test for the First Aid Merit Badge, my first badge. The doctor who was to test me was two trolleys and a bus ride away—that was pretty far. I met three other boys there, "rich" boys from the northern part of Philadelphia. They hooted at my makeshift uniform. We sat in the waiting room until the doctor was ready to quiz us. We all passed. Then the doctor, whose name I do not remember, dismissed the other three boys. When they were gone he pointed a finger at me and practically shouted: "You're going to be a doctor!"

I was so startled, I jumped in my seat. "You're going to be a doctor!" he commanded again. "Come with me."

He took me into his little office and placed a stethoscope in my hands, saying: "This is a stethoscope. We use it to listen to patients' heart beat. This is an x-ray," he said, pointing to the large, gray and white "photo" on his desk. "It's a picture of the inside of a patient's chest." He put the two ear-ends of the stethoscope into my ears, placing the bell on his chest so I could hear his heart beat. He taught me the difference between the first and second heart sounds, and he used a picture to illustrate how blood flows through the four chambers of the heart. (Thirteen years passed before I was officially taught about heart sounds in Physical Diagnosis class.)

"Come back next week," he commanded a little while later. I returned three or four times, delighted that this "important" man would spend time teaching me how to be a doctor. Each time he thrust his finger almost to my chest and boomed "You're going to be a doctor! Don't worry how," he commanded, "Don't worry about the money. Just do it!"

I don't know why he singled me out, why he gave me so much of his time. I do know that I had always dreamed of becoming a doctor and now a real doctor was telling me that my dreams would come true. This man turned my dream into reality by telling me that it could be. He didn't give me money for rent, or for heat in the winter. He didn't give me food or warm clothes. He simply told me that being a poor boy born of poor parents was not a handicap at all. He told me that I could do it. I remember, so clearly, how he emphasized that I shouldn't worry about "how to do it." Just do it.

A DIME A DOZEN

"Most of the things worth doing have been declared
impossible before they were done."
—Louis Brandeis

Writing this brings a tear of memory to my eyes, but stories like this are a dime a dozen. Baseball great Babe Ruth was born to poverty in 1895. At the age of seven he went to St. Mary's Industrial School in Baltimore, living there for much of his boyhood. That didn't stop him from becoming the home run king, and the highest paid player of his era. By the way, while Ruth was in St. Mary's, he met a poor kid named Asa Yoelson. Asa changed his name and became Al Jolson, one of the great American singers. So popular was he, they turned out all the lights on Broadway in tribute when he died. Factual reality was real clear: These two guys were going nowhere. They'd be lucky to have a steady job and a little house. Luckily, they had big dreams.

A boy was born in Russia in 1888. In 1893, his family moved to the United States, where he spent the rest of his boyhood in grinding poverty. At age sixteen or so he began working as a singing cabaret waiter in New York City's Chinatown and Bowery areas. We know that poor kid as songwriter Irving Berlin, author of "White Christmas," "God Bless America," "Alexander's Rag Time Band," the entire score to the Broadway hit "Annie Get Your Gun," and many other songs. The factual reality said that Irving couldn't make it—he barely knew how to read music. But he had a dream.

I know of an orthopedic surgeon named Serena Young, who came to the United States as a young girl in the late 1950s. Now in her mid-thirties, Dr. Young had been stricken with polio, and has been unable to walk, since she was two. Hobbling on crutches, she went to the University of California, then to medical school. When she told people that she wanted to be an orthopedic surgeon they told her she was crazy, to forget it. "Reality," remember? Today, braces holding her legs up, leaning against the operating table, she's an orthopedic surgeon. By all accounts, she's a pretty good one.

With a patchwork army, George Washington hung on to win the Revolutionary War. With a patchwork education, Thomas Edison became the greatest American inventor. With few resources other than his great dream of independence for India, one man named Ghandi stood up to the British Empire— and won. On July 25, 1989, the Wall Street Journal ran a story about two poor black brothers from the housing projects in the Bronx. Derrick and Dorian Malloy started at the bottom of the ladder at the local McDonalds. Seventeen years later, they own two Wendy's franchises that gross two and a half million dollars a year. They're not yet millionaires, but they expect to be by age forty.

The Los Angeles Times ran a front page picture and story titled "Paraplegic Gets to Top in 8-Day Yosemite Climb." His legs don't work, so Mark Wellman pulled himself up the side of El Capitan mountain in Yosemite Park. Pulling himself up to the 3,500 foot summit was the equivalent of doing 7,000 pull-ups. The crippled rock climber said "You have a dream and you know the only way that dream is going to happen is if you just do it—even if it's six inches at a time."

If you have seen television's "Happy Days," or watched the "Karate Kid" in the movie theaters, you know that Pat Morita is a good actor. You might guess that he's sitting on top of the world. You may not know that he was diagnosed as having spinal tuberculosis at the age of two, and, unable to walk, spent the next nine years in the hospital. He got out of the hospital just in time to be thrown into a Japanese-American internment camp during World War II. Pat's father was killed by a hit-and-run driver when Pat was only twenty-two. No one would have guessed that Pat would become a high-priced actor. No one, I suppose, except Pat: "If one dwells only on the hardships in life and stays in that place," he says, "that's all you will get in life. No matter what happens to a person, you have to rise above it and at least hope or dream there is a better existence. . ."

Abraham Lincoln, our sixteenth president, was born in a backwoods cabin. He had little formal education. He was a storekeeper, a postmaster, a surveyor. He even made a trip down the Mississippi to New Orleans as a flatboatman. His list of failures is legendary. He lost his job and ran unsuccessfully for the state legislature in 1832. Two years later his business failed. His sweetheart died a year after that. In 1836, he suffered a nervous breakdown. He did manage to get elected to the state legislature, but was defeated in a bid to become Speaker. In 1843, he ran unsuccessfully for Congress. In 1848, he couldn't even get nominated for Congress. His application to be Land Officer was turned down in 1848. He campaigned unsuccessfully for the Senate in 1854. He wanted to be the Vice President in 1856, but didn't get the job. He ran again for the Senate in 1858, and lost again.

Then, in 1860, one of America's greatest "failures" became President. And not just any President. Despite repeated criticism, difficulty and outright failures, he hung on to become one of our greatest Presidents.

Steven Morris, blind since birth, became musical great Stevie Wonder. John, Paul, George and Ringo were kids off the working-class streets in England. With little more than a dream and the desire, they remade the world of music as the Beatles.

Poor kids aren't the only ones with problems. A well-born boy named Humphrey seemed unable to fit in life. Poor grades and misconduct prevented him from going to Yale. Joining the Navy didn't improve matters much—he wound up in solitary, on bread and water. An injury to his mouth left him with a small speech impediment. He failed as a tugboat inspector. Finally stumbling into acting, he struggled for years before becoming the famous Humphrey Bogart.

A guy named Harland Sanders was only five when his father died. Harland dropped out of school at fourteen. After a hitch in the army, he failed as a blacksmith. By eighteen he was married. His wife announced that she was pregnant the very day he was fired from yet another job. Not much time passed before she packed up and left him. Harland dropped out of correspondence law school. Running a ferryboat or a filling station, selling tires or insurance, nothing worked out for him. At age sixty-five, he started a new business with his $105 Social Security check. The man "reality" slated for continued failure finally opened up his first Kentucky Fried Chicken, and Harland Sanders became Colonel Sanders.

Positive thoughts, positive action: PTPA. They wanted to "make it," they believed they could, so they tried. We've all heard plenty of stories about people who overcame the worst possible circumstances. These stories are a dime a dozen. What about your story?

From the Medical Literature

What happens when we slap our interpretation of reality over factual "reality?" Are we deceiving ourselves? Are we tilting with windmills or are we rewriting history before it happens? Some interesting studies suggest that our thoughts have a tremendous influence on our immune system, on how much pain we feel and other aspects of our physical, "real" being.

Researchers have shown that positive mood is associated with fewer bodily complaints.[1] This even affects the speed

1 Scheier, MF et al: *Coping with Stress: Divergent Strategies of Optimists and Pessimists.* Journal of Personality and Social Psychology, 51: 1257-1264, 1986.

with which patients recover from CABS (coronary artery bypass surgery). Positive people, who believe they will feel better soon, tend to recover quicker than those who are convinced that they are doomed to a long, painful recovery period. I've seen this happen many times in the many post-CABS patients I've treated since the surgery was first performed in the late 1960s. Just last year, a member of my extended family underwent by-pass surgery. He absolutely believed that he would recover quickly. Three days after the major surgery, in which his chest was cracked open, he was home, feeling fine.

We physicians also know that a person's belief, their interpretation of reality, can turn plain water into a powerful medicine and shrink tumors. As a physician, I believe that treating or cutting out a tumor is a good policy, especially if the tumor is caught early on in the game. I prefer to use traditional methods *plus* PTPA. But here's a story that illustrates the power of interpretation.[2]

Back in the not-so-distant 1950s, a controversial drug called Krebiozen was used in cancer therapy. One patient, a man, had a highly advanced malignancy (cancer) involving his lymph nodes. He was described as having large tumors the size of oranges in his neck, under his arms, in his chest and abdomen. The patient's doctor was giving him injections of Krebiozen. Soon the patient's tumors shrank and the fluid in his chest vanished. For over two months, the patient was symptom-free and quite enthusiastic about the Krebiozen. In the meantime, however, the AMA had conducted a study of Krebiozen. Preliminary reports appeared in the newspapers, indicating that Krebiozen was worthless for the treatment of cancer. After reading the reports, the patient became disturbed: His treatment was worthless. After two months of good health, his health deteriorated as he became depressed.

Alarmed at this turn for the worse, the physician told the

[2]Klopfer, B.: Psychological variabilities in human cancer. Journal Projective Techniques 21:331-40, 1957.

patient that Krebiozen was really good medicine. He gave the patient injections of water, but told him it was the drug. The results were amazing. The lung fluid vanished, the chest tumors melted away, and the patient who couldn't even get out of bed was now ambulatory. The water injections continued, and soon the symptom-free patient was sent home. But then the final results of the AMA study came out: Krebiozen was worthless. Within a few days the patient was admitted back to the hospital, where he rapidly failed, and died.

The "reality" is that Krebiozen is worthless. But it worked when the doctor and patient believed it would. The Krebiozen didn't mobilize the patient's immune system to fight off the tumors: The patient's belief, his interpretation of reality, gets the credit. Neither did the water beat the cancer: It was the patient's belief.

Hope is the Future

It's possible, in the midst of negativity, to fill your mind with positive thoughts. Remember: *We can't always change "factual" reality, but we can control our interpretation of reality.* Being poor but happy, filled with the desire to succeed, sure beats being poor and miserable, filled with the feeling of failure.

That feeling of success is so important. Just a few weeks ago, I flew back to Philadelphia to watch the New Year's Day parade—the Mumer's Parade, with it's colorful floats, outrageously costumed marchers, it's thousands of people packing the streets, and it's great memories. As always, my old friend Herbie and I wandered through the streets of our old neighborhood. It was great just to be back, although the neighborhood looked just as poor, and more rundown than ever. We were taking pictures of ourselves at our alma mater, Thomas Junior High School, when suddenly a basketball

sailed over the fence and rolled to a stop at our feet. I tossed
the ball back over the fence to the little group of boys, ten or
twelve year olds, playing basketball in the school yard. They
asked us who we were, and why we were taking pictures.
When I told them that Herbie and I had gone to their school,
they wanted to know how long ago.

"We graduated in 1941," I said.

"When was that?" one boy asked.

"Before your parents were born," I answered.

Then another boy asked something interesting: "Was this
a bad-ass school when you were here?"

They couldn't exactly define "bad-ass" for me, but as we
spoke, I learned that the little boys were every bit as grounded
in factual "reality" as many of my young friends had been so
many years ago. When I told them that I was a physician, they
were incredulous. The idea that anybody from their "bad-ass"
neighborhood could make it out was beyond belief.

Two generations have passed since I bounced a basketball
in the same school yard. Today's kids are of different ethnic
groups, but they are just as poor as we were, and just as certain
that there is no hope for them. To be poor is unfortunate. To
be certain that there is no hope is a disaster. Where you start
is of no consequence. The future lies in hope. The future lies
in your dreams of how wonderful things can be.

R$_x$: DREAMING UP REALITY

"First, say to yourself what you would be;
and then do what you have to do."

—Epictetus

How can we develop that hope? How can we teach
ourselves to dream? Let's look to action, "inward" and

"outward." I don't remember what happened to my yellow corduroy jacket, or that patchwork Boy Scout uniform I wore so proudly. I suppose they were passed on to someone else when I outgrew them. I no longer have my jacket or patchwork uniform, but I do have a round piece of decorative glass, hanging on my office window. Like a pie, it's cut into many pieces, each slightly tinted a different color. Bruce, my youngest, gave it to me. My wife and I arrive at the office very early every morning. I often sit in my chair looking out the window at the beautiful homes in Beverly Hills. Then the beautiful light dancing off the colored slices of glass catches my eye, and I am reminded of my old patchwork uniform, that crazy-quilt collection of cast-offs. Like my old uniform, the light is made up of a little bit of this, a little bit of that. I feel that it is especially appropriate to be reminded of my patchwork origin as I sit in my Beverly Hills office, looking at the houses belonging to the "beautiful people," just a few blocks from Rodeo Drive.

As I gaze at the patchwork light, I remember those dreams I dreamt, those crazy dreams that so many said could never come true. As I gaze at the light, I thank God for the gift of dreams. As I gaze at the light, I dream anew, knowing that the dreams I dream today make possible the reality I will live tomorrow. As I gaze at the dreamy light of hope, I say to myself:

Praise the dreamer who dreams of love,
Love the dreamer who dreams of joy,
Joy to the dreamer who dreams the dream.

Hail the dreamer who dreams of good cheer,
Cheer the dreamer who dreams of what can be.
Joy to the dreamer who dreams the dream.
Joy to the dreamer who dreams anew.

Pass It On

Now that you've begun dreaming, pass it on. Teach someone else how to look to the future with joyful anticipation. Last year a rather angry patient came to my office with a long list of ill-defined symptoms. And he was angry: mad at his boss, mad because he didn't have the education to move up, mad at the "system" that "keeps me down." After speaking with and examining the man, I sent him around the corner for some tests, then went back to the lunchroom to check the refrigerator. A little boy of about twelve years was sitting in the lunchroom munching on an apple. (We keep a basketful of apples in the waiting room for the patients.) I asked him who he was. He told me that his name was Manuel, and we got to talking. Manuel told me where he lived, and I immediately knew that it was a very poor area of Los Angeles. When he told me that his father was a janitor and his mother a maid, I realized that he was the angry man's son. As we spoke, it was clear that young Manuel didn't have much hope for the future. He looked down as we talked. He slumped down in his chair. His voice lacked energy. He spoke about the fact that his family had always been poor, and that no one from his neighborhood amounted to much.

"What do you want to be when you grow up?" I asked.

For the first time in our conversation he looked me in the eye. Just for a moment there was a light in his eyes and hope in his voice as he answered: "I want to be a doctor." Then the light faded from his eye, the energy from his body. He looked down again, saying in a voice laced with defeat: "But that's dumb. Only rich people get to be doctors."

Could it work again? I jumped to my feet, pointed my finger at him and said in my most commanding voice: "You're going to be a doctor!"

He looked as startled as I probably did fifty years ago.

"You're going to be a doctor!" I said again. "Come with me."
I grabbed Manuel by the hand and lead him back to my office,
where I put a stethoscope into his hands.

"This is a stethoscope," I explained. "You can hear a
patient's heart beat with this." I put the ear plugs into his ears,
the bell against my chest. "Can you hear it?" I asked. "Listen.
. .lub-dub, lub-dub, lub-dub. Two sounds for each heart beat."

I showed him an x-ray and an electrocardiogram, an
ophthalmoscope and a blood pressure cuff. I had him measure
my blood pressure. I had him blow into a tube connected to a
machine that gauged the strength of his lungs. I had him sit in
my chair at my desk, a stethoscope around his neck, and
imagine what it would be like to be a doctor.

"You're going to be a doctor!" I said again when I was
called away to see a patient. "Don't worry about how you're
going to do it, don't worry about the money or anything else.
Just do it!"

Two weeks later his father returned for a follow-up exami-
nation. Instead of an angry man, I found a happy man who
hugged me and said: "You've changed Manuel's life. All he
does is talk about being a doctor. When I told him to stop
dreaming, he said he wasn't dreaming, he was going to be a
doctor." The father's eyes filled with tears as he said: "He
really believes he can make it. Thank you."

I hope that young Manuel will become a doctor. But my
fondest hope is that many years from now, old Dr. Manuel will
point his finger at a young person without hope and shout:
"You're going to be a doctor!"

Pass it on. Pass on your talents, your learning, your ideas.
Most of all, pass on your belief. Tell someone who only knows
how to look down at the mud on their feet that it's OK to
dream of great things. Tell them that dreams do come true—
but you gotta dream.

Constantly pass on belief—that's a life-long assignment.

Right now, however, pass on something concrete. Give a poor child a yellow corduroy jacket of their own. Give them a Boy Scout uniform, a Daisy sash, a baseball mitt. Give them something to dream about, something to dream for, something to dream with.

"Bewitched By A Cause"

I read in the newspaper about a boy named Dick York. Dick was raised in Chicago's North Side tenements back in the Depression. His parents didn't work often because few jobs were available. When they couldn't pay the rent, one of them had to stay in their little apartment at all times, or else the landlord would lock them out. Dick watched his father fight with other men over food they dug out of the trash. When Dick was eleven, his baby brother died. There was no money to pay for a funeral, so Dick and his father stole into a graveyard late at night, dug a hole and buried the baby in a coffin made from a shoebox.

Dick's factual reality was awful. Why then, does he say he had a happy childhood? His interpretation of reality told him that things were going to get better. And they did. Someone heard him singing, one thing lead to another, and by age fifteen, Dick was starring in a CBS network radio show called "That Brewster Boy." He grew up, played on Broadway, made some movies, then became famous as Darrin Stevens, the mortal man with the goofy grin married to the beautiful witch Samantha on TV's "Bewitched."

A terrible spinal injury left him hooked on painkillers, sleeping pills and other medicines. He collapsed on the set of "Bewitched," was taken to the hospital and tossed off the show. The next 18 months passed in a drugged haze. He managed to kick his addiction, but couldn't resurrect his acting career. Thanks to years of smoking, he developed emphysema, a deadly lung disease. The once promising young actor wound up, at age 60, broke, living on a small pension in a little bungalow. Taking just a few steps was enough to have him gasping for breath. He mostly sat in a chair, a breathing tube in his nose.

Dick's factual reality was terrible. But he was still happy, excitedly ploughing ahead with his plans to help the needy. He couldn't go anywhere but he could talk on the phone. People still remembered Darrin Stevens, so he used his celebrity to help the poor. He became a one-man whirlwind, talking to bureaucrats, social workers, charities and politicians. He got on radio talkshows to spread the word. He got 15,000 changes of Army surplus clothing. He arranged for thousands of cots and blankets to be taken out of storage and put into the hands of the poor. When he heard that the homeless needed underwear, he managed to have thousands of pairs of pantyhose sent to a shelter. The Salvation Army received 5,000 cans of orange juice concentrate, thanks to Dick York.

Dick describes himself as an "old has-been actor with a hose up his nose." I describe him as living proof that factual reality often has little to do with anything. With nothing but a dream and determination, he's feeding thousands of people. Crippled, broke, unable to take more than a few steps, looking at certain death, he's joyfully laying plans to help more. Who knows? Maybe, thanks to Dick, some kid has just been given a yellow corduroy jacket with a zipper in front and three buttons on each sleeve.

Filling in the Equation

Life is a patchwork quilt, made up of all the things that

happen to us, and all the things we think. Every fact, every interpretation becomes part of our patchwork quilt. Some facts we can change, others we can't. But we can usually shape our interpretation of the facts. And when we change our interpretation of what's happening, we change the course of our lives. Changing our interpretation of what has happened can change the reality of what will happen. A little kid who learns to look at life with a smile instead of a frown can beat any odds. A boy who eats from the garbage to stay alive can become a famous actor. A crippled actor can feed and clothe thousands.

It's a negative/positive equation. A poor kid who barely reads music becomes a great songwriter. A cripple climbs a mountain. An infant stricken with crippling polio becomes a surgeon. It's all in the equation. You start with a long list of terrible negatives, yet you wind up with a longer list of positives. All you have to add is a dream.

Dreaming works if you want it to. All you have to do to make it work is to be willing to smile, and to believe.

CHAPTER THREE

RACHEL'S DREAM

"All men of action are dreamers"
—James Huneker

Fate was not kind to little Rachel. Only four months old when her mother died of tuberculosis, she was sent to live with an aunt three states away. Her older brother and sister were farmed out to other relatives, while her father remained home in Ohio, trying to earn a living. That was not easy, for the Depression was raging. An aunt cannot replace a mother, of course, but Rachel was happy with her new family. She was treated well, there was enough money to keep her well-fed and warm, she had toys to play with, and was surrounded by countless loving aunts, uncles and cousins. Rachel was the family's little doll, the youngest of all the cousins, a happy child who smiled and laughed a lot. Once a month Rachel's aunt took her on the "bank tour." They spent an entire day going from bank to bank, depositing a dollar here, a dollar there. The aunt, who had lost her savings when the banks failed, spread her money around, just to be sure.

Rachel's father remarried, so at the age of five, the young girl was sent back to Ohio. The family was together. Her father had a job. Rachel soon had a best friend, Sally. There was even, occasionally, enough money for Rachel to take a trolly to school. Of course, if she walked to school instead, she could use the trolly fare to buy a Hershey bar, a rare, heavenly treat. Rachel told me how a Hershey bar was to be savored.

You did not chew the chocolate, no: You bit a little chunk off, and you held it in your mouth. As the chocolate melted, you moved it around your mouth with your tongue, coating the insides of your lips and the roof of your mouth with warm liquid chocolate.

Unfortunately, Rachel's new mother was the proverbial wicked stepmother. Perhaps wicked is not the right word; she was emotionally disturbed. She was sick. She vented her anger, which no one understood, on Rachel and her siblings. Rachel's brother, ten years older, was strong enough to defend himself. In any case, he did not remain in the family house for long. Rachel's older sister, a tough tomboy, suffered physically and emotionally, but never backed down. Rachel, however, was a sensitive girl, a quiet girl unable to protect herself from her stepmother's reasonless wrath. Often time, for no discern-able reason, the stepmother would charge into the girls' room, swinging a cat o'nine tails. If they didn't jump out the window quickly enough, Rachel and her sister were beaten. The step-mother often locked the children and their father out of the house all night during the cold Ohio winter. They slept, huddled together, in their father's truck. One wonderful day Rachel had a birthday party—an honest-to-goodness birthday party with friends, decorations, a cake, even a few little pres-ents. Rachel was, as she says, "in her glory," she was sitting on top of the world. But just after her friends left, the stepmother began screaming about the mess. She grabbed little Rachel and began pounding her head against the wall. Holding the little girl by the hair, pounding her head against the wall, the stepmother slowly moved her toward a big nail sticking out of the wall. Just before Rachel's head was slammed into the nail, her older sister seized their stepmother and threatened to hit her with a large pan. Rachel fled, hiding in the garage.

Why didn't Rachel's father protect his children? He was a very kind and gentle man, much like his youngest daughter.

He was no match for the mentally-ill woman he married. Even when he felt strong enough to stand up to her, she quickly knocked him down to size by threatening to turn him in. He was, you see, an illegal immigrant who lived in constant fear of being deported.

This being the Depression, Rachel and her family never knew if there'd be any food for dinner. They moved often, barely one step ahead of the bill collectors. Still, there were happy times. There were simple joys like reading. They laughed at her and called her a bookworm, but Rachel loved to read. Every week she got new books from the library. Perhaps books took her away from life, if only for a few hours. And there were friends, good friends like Sally. When she speaks ·of her childhood, which is rare, Rachel mentions her kind father, reading, Hershey bars, and her friend Sally. Although she had an impish sense of humor, Rachel was very quiet and shy, the kind of girl that could be there yet not be noticed. She probably developed that trait in self-defense: The more invisible she was at home, the safer she felt. She also had a strong sense of duty. She had always shined her father's shoes every week because she wanted him to look good. Years later, on her wedding day, in her white gown, she shined his shoes again just as she'd always done.

No, fate was not kind to little Rachel, though it did give her a special gift: Her ability to dream. She told us that she had hundreds of dreams, one for every occasion. When her birthday passed without a party, without a present, she dreamed of the wonderful birthday parties she would throw for her children. When she went to bed hungry, she dreamed of the huge banquets she would have for her family and friends. When her stepmother beat her cruelly, she dreamed of having a little girl of her own, one to love and protect. "When things were bad," she told us, "I'd dream of how good it would be, someday."

For every problem life threw at her, Rachel had a dream. For every dream destroyed, she had a new one. And most of all, she had the dream her aunt gave her. "She told me that now, as a child, I had little control over things. But soon I would be an adult, and I could make my world the way I wanted it to be."

Little Rachel, the shy, frightened, abused girl, was a dream factory. Now, a mother of her own and adopted children, as well as a grandmother of five, she says, "Dreaming was the only way I could fight back." "Especially," she added, "when my stepmother told me what a rotten good-for-nothing I was, when she made me feel like a failure, I fought back by dreaming of doing something."

Like Mitchel, the pilot; like Sally, the Concentration Camp survivor; like Mark, the little ballplayer who finally became a hero—Rachel was a fighter, a winner. Her weapon was an endless supply of dreams. It didn't matter if one was dashed, she had a thousand more.

Dream A Little Dream

Back in medical school, we were taught that dreams were for the psychiatrists to worry about; our job was to be scientific. Well, good as science is, it has yet to unravel the powerful mysteries of dreaming. Those pictures we put into our heads, those projections of what we want to happen, are very real, and have a very real effect on us. How can a dream, a piece of illusion, change our biochemistry, alter our immune system, and make the downtrodden powerful? It all sounds like nonsense. It's not scientific.

A few words about "scientific." Science is an excellent tool, a wonderful approach to learning. The scientific method has helped us unravel many of nature's mysteries, to transplant hearts and send rockets to the moon. While we praise science, however, we should not lose sight of the fact that science is but one approach to learning. It's strengths are many, but limited.

When we want to put something down, we say it's "unscientific." Well, the fact that the scientific method cannot explain something does not mean that something is bad, or useless. To say that something is unscientific simply means that science cannot explain it. There's nothing wrong with the "something." The fault lies with science's inadequacies. Things that are unscientific are not, by definition, good or bad. They are, for now, and possibly forever, beyond the realm of science.

Dreams are unscientific because, so far, they have defied science to dissect and define them. Yet, as a physician, I can tell you that dreams are very powerful. Barry and I have written about many, many patients whom I believe survived only because they dared to dream that they would. It may not be terribly scientific, but I say go ahead, dream a little dream. Dream a big dream. Dream a thousand dreams.

The Science of Dreams

Having said that if dreams are unscientific it is the fault of science, I'd like to point out that some researchers are beginning to turn a scientific eye at the mysteries of the mind. Researchers at UCLA worked with a group of actors, who were instructed to play happy and sad scenes. Acting, like dreaming, is a form of pretending.

These were "method" actors and they threw themselves into their parts. They wanted to "become" the person they were playing, to feel, smell, touch, breathe and see everything their character would.

The actors were asked to play out "happy" and "sad" scenes. Their secretory immunoglobulin A or IgA, an indication of immune-system strength, was measured. IgA is an antibody found in the mouth and elsewhere that protects the respiratory tract and other parts of the body.

When the actors played out the "happy" scenes, their IgA went up. But when they acted out the "sad" scenes, it went down. Acting/dreaming boosted and battered their immune systems. As my professors told me back in medical school, the psyche plays a large role in our physical health, even if we're acting the part.

Back in 1979 one of my patients, a well-known and very beautiful actress, came to see me complaining of anxiety, palpitations, headaches and other problems. It was obvious that she was suffering the adverse effects of stress, but where was the stress coming from? I went with her to the movie set out in Burbank, just over the Hollywood Hills from Beverly Hills. There, in the center of a large, dusty, airplane-like hanger, was a sumptuous bedroom set surrounded by chairs, cameras and other equipment. Actors, electricians, assistants, camera people, gofers and plenty of other people were standing around, eating, drinking, talking, and for the most part looking quite bored. I thought that being on the set was exciting, but it was old hat to them.

My patient came out, glamorously dressed for her role, and sat with me by the set. I had brought some of the equipment with me, so while they were shooting a scene without her, I checked her blood pressure, heart rate, and ran an EKG (electrocardiogram). I checked her muscle tension using an electrode on her forehead. I measured the temperature of her fingers, the sweat and electrical impedance of her hands, and did some blood studies.

Then the director called for her, and she went onto the set. There the male lead was laying in bed, supposedly asleep. As

I watched, fascinated, my patient acted out a scene in which she grew furious and stabbed him to death. I knew it was a movie, but she was so good I believed her. The director yelled "cut" and she quickly came back to our seats just off the set so I could reevaluate her. Her hands were cold, wet, and trembling. Her blood pressure was elevated. She had a tachycardia (rapid heart beat). The temperature of the skin of her fingers had dropped by over 20 degrees Fahrenheit. The electrical conductivity of her skin had changed. Her muscle tension was markedly increased. These and other measurements showed that this actress played her part so well, she fooled her body as well as her audiences. Her body reacted to the danger and emotions she was pretending to feel. Her make-believe turned her body chemistry upside down in no time at all. And some of those changes had long-lasting, negative effects on her health. But it was all a dream.

We're not actors. We can't play the happy and sad scenes the way they do. But we are dreamers, and in our dreams we are all the greatest actors of all. Let's take action. Let's dream the dream. These positive thoughts can lead to positive actions.

No Dreams to Dream

A beautiful woman came to my office recently one morning, complaining of stomach and back pains. After taking her complete personal and medical history, and examining her, I sat down with her in my office to talk. The conversation had hardly begun before she said "I'm a failure." (I shudder when I hear people say that.) The woman, Alicia, told me she was forty-five today, and immediately broke into tears. When she composed herself, she told me that she had given up a small but successful business to come to Los Angeles and marry a man, that the marriage only lasted three years, that the divorce was bitter, that her attempt to start a new business failed, and on and on. "I'm a failure," she said several times.

When I asked her what she dreamed about, Alicia looked at me as if I were speaking Martian. "Dream? I don't dream about anything."

"What great things do you want to do?" I asked.

"I can't do anything great. Failures like me have nothing to dream about."

Was Alicia a failure? Well, her marriage and her second business failed. But her first business had succeeded. As we continued to talk, she admitted that she had succeeded many times in her life. True, she had some major setbacks, but she was not a failure. The problem was in her perception. She *believed* that she was a failure.

Alicia wasn't a failure; she was an actor playing the role of a failure, acting out an unhappy scene over and over again. She played through the unhappy scene, and now she couldn't put the script down. She played the terrible scene over and over, never turning the page to move on to the next scene, never picking up a new script.

Bring Up the Curtain on Success

Each and every one of us has failed at some time in our lives, but we are not failures. People often bare their soul to their doctors. Many have tearfully told me that they are absolute, miserable failures in every possible way. When we carefully go through their lives, however, we find that they're not failures at all. They're just actors so caught up in an unhappy scene, they forget to turn the page. I have yet to speak to someone who didn't do at least one good thing in their life, who can't turn to a better page in their script. And I have yet to meet someone who, if I can get them to think about their one success, doesn't start doing better.

I told Alicia that even a long string of mistakes and setbacks does not mean you're a failure. And even if you're a failure in one area such as business or in marriage, there are other areas. Life is multifaceted. If you think about it, even the most "successful" person in the world will probably fail at more things than he or she will succeed at. I know a great computer programmer who can barely write a complete sentence, and is out-played in any sport you can name by ten-year olds. I know a very "successful" movie director whose kids hate him because he is intolerable. I'm a "successful" Beverly Hills physician, yet I have trouble doing anything more technical than screwing in a light bulb. I had to have Barry come over to show me how to work the new electric alarm clock my wife bought. Given our different talents and inclinations, we all do well in some areas, and not so well in others.

The Technical Track to Where?

Back in high school, we had three "tracks:" College bound, business, and technical. Technical was for the kids the school didn't think were very bright. I was in technical. I took wood shop, metal shop, electric shop, and every other shop there was. I couldn't make anything. I couldn't saw wood straight, I couldn't hammer a nail, I couldn't make the metal bend right. One day in electric shop, I short-circuited everything. I just didn't blow out the power at my table, I blew out the power for the entire shop. I was so inept that I was dangerous. The teacher used to give me a nickel to stay out of class. And that's not the only class I was kicked out of. I once spent a whole month sitting on a bench outside the principal's office in elementary school. I wasn't allowed to return to class until my mother came to speak to the principal. But she had a mean right hook, so I wasn't about to tell her I was sitting on the bench. I might still be sitting there if a neighbor hadn't seen me and told my mother.

Am I a success? I've snatched people back from the brink of death, true, but, like all physicians, I've made my share of errors. I get along great with some of my children while, with others, the relationship is in progress. Some of my children are "positive" kids with a great deal of belief in themselves, while some are still struggling. I've built up a thriving medical practice, but then again, I've been taken by some shrewd, and some not-so-shrewd, con men. I've made lots of money, but I've lost plenty. There was a time when it looked as if we were going to lose it all. If you add it all up, I've probably failed more times than I've succeeded in life.

The script of my life is filled with failures and unhappy scenes. There are also success-filled and joyful scenes. When I come to a difficult scene, I play my part then turn the page. When I come to a happy scene I savor my role, and I remember it. Am I a success? Yes, but only because I focus on the good things I've done. I look at the unhappy things (I hope I learn from them), then I look to the good. I look forward to the future with eyes filled with past success.

A crippled man dreams of climbing a tall mountain. A little girl tormented by a demented step-mother dreams of making her own children happy. A little boy stuck in wood shop dreams of becoming a doctor. They were dreamers. They were actors playing scenes in the theater of their mind, scenes that had not yet been written. They were writing the scenes they wanted to play in the future. They dreamed a little dream of great things.

Failures are simply those who have gotten stuck in the unhappy scenes. A failure can turn into a success by dropping the curtain, turning the page, then bringing the curtain up again on a new scene. And even as you play through the rough parts, keep dreaming about the good parts to come.

Always A Dream

If we're actors, we're also writers. Dreams are our pens. Little Rachel was a prolific writer, she had a thousand dreams, one for every occasion. Others only write one scene, replaying and refining it over and over. But what if you don't have a dream, like Alicia? Many people who have been battered by life ask me what they could possibly dream about. "All my hopes were shattered," one woman told me. "My husband and my children were killed in a car wreck. I had a leg cut off. The guy who hit us was uninsured. My husband's life insurance company is still holding up my money on a technicality. I lost my home, I've got nothing. What could I dream about?"

I have a small insight into how this woman feels, for I, too, have lost a child. I know that it is often hard to tear ourselves away from the unhappy scenes. I know that we tend to get stuck, and we can't believe that there is anything but more misery ahead. When you're standing over your child's grave, watching the casket drop down into the ground, what can you possibly dream about?

Not too many years ago, a woman named Candy Lightner lost a child to a drunk driver. Candy dreamed of getting drunk drivers off the road so that other parents would not have to bury their children. Candy's dream launched MADD (Mother's Against Drunk Driving). Her dream made a big difference. Her dream has saved many lives by helping to change our laws and attitudes toward drunk drivers. From the greatest despair I can imagine came Candy's dream. Her dream gave people everywhere a great treasure: Lives saved because fewer drunks are on the road.

There's always a good dream to dream. The greatest dreams can spring from the blackest nights.

WHAT DREAM CAN YOU DREAM?

*"I feel that the greatest reward for doing
is the opportunity to do more."*
—Jonas Salk

Alicia said she had no dream to dream. When people tell me they don't know what to dream about, I ask them:

- *What do you care about?*
- *What brings a tear to your eye?*
- *What quickens your pulse?*
- *What makes you smile?*
- *What makes you feel good about yourself, how can you get others to feel the same?*
- *What injustice makes you want to help others?*
- *What gets you to thinking, "if only. . .?"*
- *What do you look forward to?*
- *What do you remember fondly?*
- *What do you wish you could do?*
- *As a kid, what did you love to do?*
- *What did you want to be when you grew up?*
- *What is it you wish you had done for a loved one who has passed away?*
- *What do you wish everyone would do for their loved ones, before they pass away?*
- *How would you make a sad kid smile?*
- *What would you like to do for the underprivileged?*
- *What are your plans for making this country, or this world, a better place to live?*

I sit down with my patients, asking them questions like these. Their answers usually give them the dream. If they still can't think of a dream, I tell them what my parents dreamed of: A better life for me, their only child. My parents fulfilled their dream by working extra shifts, by trying to help me with homework which they themselves did not understand, by saving their pennies to buy me a baseball mitt or a Boy Scout cap, by encouraging me to reach for the stars. They never made much money, they were never leaders of men, they never invented anything, but they were great successes.

Every parent who sacrifices to put a smile on their child's face is a great success. Every grown child who takes care of an elderly parent is a success. Everybody who helps anybody, who leaves the world a slightly better place, is a great success.

Success is easy to come by. Just pursue your great dream of helping others. Dreams are easy to come by. There are thousands of dreams locked up inside of you. Let one go, chase it to the ends of the earth, and you'll be a great success.

Dreaming the Long Night Through

Candy Lightner held onto her MADD dream for a long time, through great difficulties, before it came to fruition. How long can one hold a dream? On February 23, 1991, the Los Angeles Times ran an article called "The Downstairs Diva." It seems that a woman named Ealynn Voss, the only child of poor German immigrants, wanted to be an opera singer. After graduating college she went to the various auditions, even traveling through Europe in the mid-1970s looking for parts to play. No one offered her a job so she wound up in Malibu, California, working as a nanny.

She watched the children, she cooked, she scrubbed the floors. She described how, at the end of every tiring day, she stared out at the ocean feeling "a sense of great discouragement."

Despite the discouragement, she never surrendered her dream. If she couldn't be a great opera singer, she could at least answer an ad for a part-time director of the local church choir. She got the job, and she sang some solos at another church. A retired opera singer heard her, and he caught her dream. For six years, the retired singer and his wife worked with Ealynn and trained her. When they felt she was ready, they sent recordings of her to their old contacts. It worked.

In 1988 the nanny-singer traveled through the United States, Europe and Australia. Today, at age forty-one, her childhood dream has finally come true. She debuted in the Los Angeles Music Center Opera performance of Richard Strauss' "Elektra." She's scheduled to sing with the New York City Opera and has another big contract for 1993, singing "Aida" with the Los Angeles Music Center Opera.

Growing up poor never stopped her from dreaming. The fact that she couldn't get a job singing never stopped her from dreaming. Fourteen years of watching children and scrubbing floors never stopped her from dreaming of being a great opera star. The pages kept turning. The curtain has gone up on a great new scene in Eaylnn's life. The spotlight is now on her because she never stopped dreaming.

Ealynn's not the only one who knows how to hold onto a dream. Right below her article is a story about two "swings." Swings are actors who understudy every single role in a play. These two swings, Kerrianne Spellman and Daniel Friedman, have memorized every line, every step, every note sung for 27 different roles in the great musical play, "Les Miserables." They usually don't know what role they're going to play until they walk into the theatre shortly before the curtain goes up, until they see which actor didn't make it. They'd like to be lead players, not everyone's understudy. But until then, they dream of what might be.

Running the Race

History is full of dreamers who never gave up their dream, no matter how many times failure struck them. Mahatma Gandhi labored for years to free his country. Martin Luther King fought and died for his great dream. When I was a young boy, a man named Glen Cunningham was running out his dream. Cunningham, the great American miler of the 1930s, suffered severe burns to his leg in a schoolhouse fire when he was a boy. They wondered if he would walk again. Well, he walked, then he ran. He set high school, then college, then national and then world records for the mile. He represented the United States twice in the Olympics, winning a Silver Medal in 1936. Why would a boy who was not supposed to walk again dream of being a world-class runner? Why not?

Barry and I have run several "mini marathons" at UCLA, the Rose Bowl, Century City and other parts of Los Angeles. At every race, we runners are divided into categories according to age and sex. There's usually another category: The wheelchair runners. These guys and girls have lost the use of their legs, but they're out there in specially-designed wheelchairs, "going for the gold." At one 10-kilometer race, Barry joined everyone else in a standing ovation as a white-haired, 70ish woman crossed the finish line.

We know someone else who is racing, trying to see her dream become reality before her eyes close forever. Debra is a woman who, like little Rachel, was severely abused by a demented stepmother. Like Rachel, Debra dreamed of lavishing love on her own children, giving them everything she was denied. Unfortunately Debra, who married late, was unable to bear children. After many years of trying, but before they could adopt, her husband died, leaving her quite poor.

But Debra never stopped dreaming. If she couldn't have children of her own, she could dream a new dream. She could volunteer to help with the Special Olympics. That's how this childless woman became everyone's mother. She said that although she missed the special joys of having her own children, she had the never-ending joy of watching so many kids become winners, year after year. And everyone was a winner, every time, she added.

I wish I could end the story here, but it doesn't have such a simple, happy ending. You see, Debra had noted stomach pains and other problems for some time. When she finally went to the doctor, she was told that she had stomach cancer. Her physician told her that she had three months to live.

I'm a physician, I've diagnosed many patients with cancer, but I could never tell them that they had six months to live, or two months, or five years, or what have you. I know all the averages. I also know that there is no such thing as the "average" patient. Each one is an individual. Each will live for a greater or lesser amount of time, depending on many factors, including their beliefs and their desires.

Belief battled with desire in Debra. She was a firm believer in modern medicine. She really believed her doctor when he said she had three months to live. But Debra was working with one particular handicapped girl, a little angel named Lindsey who looked as if she could be the daughter Debra never had. "More than anything," she said, "I want to see Lindsey run in a stadium full of people, I want to see her cross the finish line, I want to cry with pride when I pin a ribbon on her."

The Special Olympics were six months away. That Debra believed she would die in three months was a terrible blow. Believing you will die is like pouring a million more germs into an open wound. Luckily, her desire to hang on until Lindsey crossed the finish line overwhelmed her terrible belief. When I asked her how she got through the pain, she told me that the secret was to look into the future, and to see how wonderful it was going to be. She said that she developed this technique when she was a child, battered by her stepmother. "The worse it got the tighter I closed my eyes and saw how good it would be one day," she explained. "Since the things I saw with my eyes open were so bad, I looked at the good things in the future with my eyes closed." This amazing woman described how she taught Lindsey to "see with her eyes closed, because that's when you see the clearest."

"What do you mean, that's when you see the clearest?" I asked.

"With your eyes closed you can eliminate all the distractions and just see the future as you want it."

Despite the great pain and weakness that gripped her almost from the moment the doctor announced that she was doomed, Debra worked with Lindsey several times a week. As Debra struggled to remain alive, so, apparently, did young Lindsey. I don't know what Lindsey was suffering from, but it sent her to the hospital three times in six months. Three harrowing trips that left the little girl exhausted, with hardly enough energy to walk. Still, the woman and the girl practiced for the games, the one wanting to win a ribbon, the other determined to pin it on her little friend. Debra told me that although her original dream of having children to love never came true, her new dream was just as good.

I saw Debra in the hospital just two weeks before the Special Olympics. I don't know what was hurting her more: the cancer, the treatment, or her doctor's insistence that she was going to die very soon. Luckily, she had an incredible desire to live, at least until the games.

I knew Debra was going to make it when I heard that this quite, very docile patient had literally screamed at her physician, demanding that he stop telling her she was going to die. She shouted something like "Damn it! You're not taking my dream away from me! Get out of here!"

Her desire to see her dream come true swept away her belief that she wouldn't make it. She immediately began to improve, and was soon out of the hospital. She was very weak and she was advised to stay in the hospital, but she insisted on taking her place as Lindsey's coach at the Special Olympics. The brave little girl ran the race, and the brave older woman pinned on the ribbon. Everybody was a winner that day, especially the woman whose dream, whose new dream, came true.

R$_x$: SEEING WITH YOUR EYES CLOSED

Dreaming is acting. It's also seeing the future you want to be yours. It's seeing yourself as you would like to be, where you would like to be, and how you would like to be. Dreaming is seeing with your eyes closed. Everyday, dream your dream. When things are good, when things are bad; when you're happy, when you're sad; when you're rich, when you're poor; when you're on the brink of success, when you're in the midst of failure, dream your dream.

At least once a day, preferably three or four times, see your future. See it with your eyes closed. Find a quiet room, a comfortable chair, unplug the phone, loosen your clothing and dream your dreams. When you're finished, keep one image in mind, focus on a mental picture of something wonderful as you say:

I see sunlight and joy,
With my eyes closed.
And what I see, can be.

I see laughter and love,
With my eyes closed.
And what I see, will be.

I see future before me,
With my eyes closed.
And what I see, is.

Remember Mary Lou Retton, the little gymnast who won America's first ever gold medal for women's gymnastics in the 1984 Olympics? She used to dream a lot, dream of winning. She would see herself jumping, twisting, flying through air and landing perfectly. She would see the score board light up with a perfect "10." She would see her parents and coach applauding her. She would see the medal she had won. And she would see the big Wheaties contract slapped into her hand. She saw her future regularly.

It's an old technique, but a good one. Many top-notch athletes include dreaming as part of their training. They close their eyes and see themselves executing the moves perfectly. A basketball study showed how effective the technique can be. Guys were divided into three groups, and told that they would participate in a contest to see who could make the most baskets. The first group was told to practice throwing baskets. The second group was told to practice in their heads, to see themselves throwing baskets. The third group was given no special instructions. At the appointed time, all three groups were tested. The second group, the one that saw with their eyes closed, did the best.

Years ago some of my colleagues insisted I golf with them. My golf "game" consists of eventually hitting the little white ball, then spending a lot of time looking for it. I'm obviously not a good golfer, yet I've taught many very good golfers how to improve their game by practicing in their head.

ACTION WITH YOUR EYES WIDE OPEN

> ". . . the dream of yesterday is the hope of
> today and reality of tomorrow."
> —Robert H. Goddard

Now that you can see it, do it! Couple your positive thoughts with positive action. Strengthen your positive thoughts with positive actions. Write out your answers to these questions:

- *What do you care about?*
- *What brings a tear to your eye?*
- *What quickens your pulse?*
- *What makes you smile?*
- *What makes you feel good about yourself, how can you get others to feel the same?*
- *What injustice makes you want to help others?*
- *What gets you to thinking, "if only. . .?"*
- *What do you look forward to?*
- *What do you remember fondly?*
- *What do you wish you could do?*
- *As a kid, what did you love to do?*
- *What did you want to be when you grew up?*
- *What is it you wish you had done for a loved one who has passed away?*
- *What do you wish everyone would do for their loved ones, before they passed away?*
- *How would you make a sad kid smile?*
- *What would you like to do for the underprivileged?*
- *What are your plans for making this country, or this world, a better place to live?*

Most people will find their dream somewhere in these

answers. Maybe your dream concerns yourself, or maybe it deals with others. Perhaps it's a new dream. Perhaps it's an old dream that never came true. It may be something you can do yourself or it may require help. Whatever the case may be, whatever your dream, see it with your eyes closed, then try to make it come true. And if you pursue your dream for a lifetime but it never comes true, you're still a success, because most of the fun is in trying.

Little Rachel's dream came true and so can yours. See it with your eyes closed, see it so well that it becomes real.

CHAPTER FOUR

TOGETHER

"Both together is best of all."
—English Proverb

As a little boy, I spent a lot of time with my stern but good-natured grandfather. He took a special interest in me, perhaps because out of all his grandchildren, I had the least. In my earliest memories he's already in his sixties, standing about five foot eight or nine, with a white moustache in the center of his round face. He had worked hard all his life, and boy, was he strong. People would bet him that he couldn't lift up a one-hundred pound sack of potatoes. He'd bet that he could carry *two* sacks down to the corner. He always won the bet.

Grandfather had been a peasant in the old country. In the United States, he had two trades: He had a little family farm in New Jersey, and he was a shoemaker in Philadelphia. But it seemed to me as if he spent most of his time helping the poor. He felt that we all owed it to each other, and to God, to do good. Back then, there were no official charities, at least none that I was aware of. The poor just got poorer. Grandfather collected clothes for the poor, though he had little for himself. I remember going with him, in his old truck, to pick up bread from the bakeries around 4th and South in South Philly. That was quite an adventure for a little boy, riding in one of the very few trucks on the streets back then. These were the days when the milkman came around every morning with a horse and wagon, when vegetable sellers pushed their carts through the streets yelling "potatoes" and "apples," when the knife sharpener pushed a cart with his grindstone from door to door. I remember the young man, probably in his mid-twenties, who walked down the street, a dozen or so brooms on his shoulders, yelling "Brooms, brooms, buy your brooms." The streets were alive with people, with commerce, with play. I remember the doctor walking from house to house. He had a car, one of the very rare private cars, but he always walked.

Well, Grandfather and I would pick up big barrels of day-old bread, bread the bakers couldn't sell. He'd hoist those barrels onto his truck, then we'd drive all around the neighborhood, bringing bread to the poor. All the bakers knew Grandfather. So did the poor people. As I recall, the bakers, who were giving, were as glad to see Grandfather as were the poor people, who were receiving. They took great joy in giving.

Grandfather, who had little, kept telling me, who had nothing, that there was nothing as rewarding as giving. Back then, in stores and houses, people kept all sorts of cans, large tin cans with holes in them. Grandfather had several of these cans in his kitchen. The idea was to put money in the cans, and every so often someone collected the money to buy coal for the poor in the winter, to buy them clothes, to feed them, to send the very sick ones to the country, and so on. "Life has meaning when we help each other," he would say. "Every time we help each other, we give meaning to our lives."

Grandfather was very strong in this belief. Many people told him that he was foolish to waste his time on charity when he could be making more money for himself and his family, but Grandfather felt he had a duty, that we all had a duty. A deeply religious man, he often said that the world made sense to him. He knew who his Creator was. He knew what his duty was, and he knew that he could do it. It was that simple. He always told me to do good for the sake of doing good, not because you want to be rewarded in this life or the next. It's

nice if you get a reward, but don't worry about it. Do good for
the sake of doing good.

"Duty," "giving meaning to our lives," "helping each
other:" These are old fashioned ideas. But to Grandfather
these were simply life's guiding concepts. Grandfather's devo-
tion to charity gave meaning to his life. He wasn't just a poor
farmer and shoemaker; he was also part of the grand scheme
of life. When someone he had fed later did something
wonderful, Grandfather felt as if they had done it together.
When a child he clothed during a cold winter grew up and
married, Grandfather rejoiced as if it were his wedding. When
the pennies he put into the charity cans paid for the doctor to
deliver a baby, Grandfather felt as if he had a new grandchild.

For Grandfather, there was no such thing as an impossible
problem. He always encouraged me to stay in school, to graduate high school. (That was pretty big stuff in my
neighborhood.) He even dared to say that I could go to college,
to medical school, law school, whatever I wanted. "Go," he
would say. "Don't worry about anything, just go. Somebody
like me will make sure you have bread to eat. You and I,
together, will become a doctor."

He was right. Many times when I was down and out,
ready to quit, somebody "gave me bread." When I was a poor
student, with little money to feed my wife and children, let
alone pay tuition, I used to sell pharmaceuticals to the doctors.
I had my own tiny company, and our entire inventory fit in one
box. I must have been crazy, trying to compete with the big
companies. One day, broke as usual, I went to City Hall to
make a sealed bid to sell medicine to a city hospital. All the
sealed bids were entered into a ledger by the man who stood
behind a counter. The lowest bid would get the contract.
Every other company had already bid, I was the last. I chatted
with the man, whom I had never seen before, for a few
minutes. When it came time for me to make my bid, he

opened the ledger to the proper page, and turned it around so that I couldn't help seeing the figures. He then walked to the window, returned and asked if I was ready to bid. I bid exactly one penny below the lowest bid listed. I got the contract.

Why did he risk his job to help me? I wouldn't be surprised if the big companies had tried to bribe him, but he stuck his neck out to help me—and got nothing but my unspoken gratitude in return. Why did he do it? Perhaps he felt he had a duty.

Many people have helped me through the years. I didn't know most of them and I don't know why they chose to help me. I can only assume that they, like Grandfather, felt they had an obligation to their fellow man. Although Grandfather died before I finished medical school, he and I, together with all those who helped me, became a doctor.

"NICE" Versus "FUD"

Life was never easy for Grandfather, but everything made sense to him. He knew who he was, and what was expected of him. Grandfather felt like a part of his community. He touched, through his charity work, every part, every person. Every joy was his to share and every sorrow was his, as well. Giving gave great depth and meaning to his life. He never gave a thought to the future. Aside from the fact that he thought he'd live forever, he knew in his heart that when he could no longer take care of himself, there would be somebody to give him bread. His life was always new, interesting and challenging. He had a great sense of belonging.

Compare Grandfather to the brilliant, mostly young scientists who sent man into space. In the late 1960s and 1970s, as our space program basked in the glow of one success after another, the engineers at Cape Canaveral/Cape Kennedy and their families were the nation's leaders in divorce, drinking, drug abuse and sudden death due to heart attacks. The better our rockets performed, the worse their creators fared. The rocket scientists were not overburdened with the standard risk factors (elevated cholesterol, cigarette smoking, elevated blood pressure, diabetes, obesity), yet they were dropping at an alarming rate. So much so, our government wondered if the Russians weren't trying to destroy our space program by poisoning our scientists.

I recently spent several hours speaking with Robert Elliot, M.D., the man the U.S. government hired to figure out what was happening. I was looking forward to meeting him at a conference we were both scheduled to speak at, the *Clinically Relevant Risk Factor Management of Cardiac Disease* workshop in Springfield, Missouri. We drove in together from the airport, so we had a great chance to talk. He told me that it was a matter of NICE turning into FUD.

Our rocket engineers were under a great deal of pressure—stress—to beat the Russians. But it was NICE stress: a *N*ew, *I*nteresting, *C*hallenging *E*xperience. Unfortunately, every time the scientists proved their worth and took another step ahead of the Russians by firing off another rocket, our government fired a batch of them. About 15% were fired after each successful launch. According to Dr. Elliot, between 1965 and 1973, the work force at Cape Canaveral/Cape Kennedy was chopped in half. They'd work hard, they'd solve intricate problems of physics and engineering, they'd wow the world, then they'd be out of a job. One day they're the nation's well-paid, highly-respected best and brightest, the next day they're bagging groceries at a local market. Their formerly NICE environment became filled with FUD: *F*ear, *U*ncertainty, and *D*oubt.

The rocket engineers checked out OK on their physical examinations and laboratory tests, and the standard coronary risk factors were not unusually high. The ones who had died only rarely had the blocked coronary arteries the doctors first thought were the problem. But Dr. Elliot did find an unusually high level of anxiety and depression, plus feelings of hopelessness and helplessness. They were waiting for the ax to fall. They knew that when it dropped, they would lose their job, their salary, their status and, to some degree, their identities.

After studying the autopsy reports of engineers who had suddenly dropped dead, Dr. Elliot concluded that their negative feelings lead to massive outpourings of adrenaline and other stress chemicals that destroyed a portion of the muscle fibers that make up the heart. They died from FUD: Fear, Uncertainty and Doubt.

The Science of FUD

Can fear, uncertainty and doubt really kill us, cause us to suddenly drop dead? Sure, we've all heard stories, but is there any solid evidence linking the FUD type of stress to sudden heart death?

There's plenty of evidence. When we're fearful, uncertain and filled with great doubt, our nervous system responds by flooding the body with adrenaline, cortisone and other "stress hormones." That's OK in an emergency, but over the long run they can be deadly. If you inject sleeping dogs with large amounts of adrenaline, they will die. The engineers' FUD triggered the release of large amounts of adrenaline within their bodies. If you compare microscopic pictures of the dog's hearts to the rocket engineers' hearts, you'll see the same lesions (abnormalities). Indeed, within five minutes of injecting anesthetized animals with a variety of "stress chemicals," you'll see the beginning of the same kind of heart damage that killed the engineers. You'll find similar damage in the hearts of people who have been mugged, and in test pilots who lose control of their planes. It's fear, uncertainty and doubt.

If you fill rabbits with FUD by moving them back and forth between comfortable and terribly-overcrowded cages, never giving them enough time to adjust to either, they'll drop dead within half a year. It's fear, uncertainty and doubt.

If you let an aggressive tree shrew attack a submissive shrew, then separate them but leave them within view of each other, the submissive shrew lies perfectly, fearfully still most all the time, then dies within two days to two weeks. It's fear, uncertainty and doubt.

FUD can cause our heart to beat irregularly. An excellent study conducted by Rozanski[1], reported in the prestigious New England Journal of Medicine, illustrated the relationship between mental stress and the heart.

Rozanski found myocardial ischemia (lack of oxygen to the heart muscle, a potentially deadly condition) hitting patients with coronary artery disease (CAD) who were asked to perform some potentially stressful tasks (such as public speaking, arithmetic, and emotional recall). This was silent ischemia—harmful heart changes the patients could not feel, but the doctors could monitor.

The emotional/mental stress also produced in some patients a drop in the amount of blood pumped out of the heart with each contraction (this is known as the ejection fraction). Equally frightening, the doctors found abnormal heart wall motions (contractions) in some of the patient's hearts. These dangerous, possibly deadly effects hit heart patients who were mentally/emotionally stressed.

FUD need not kill us suddenly, it can take its time, slowly increasing our risk of having a heart attack. Substances released by FUD in our body can raise our cholesterol. If you examine the cholesterol levels of pilots, you'll see that FUD set

[1]Rozanski, A et al.: *Mental Stress and the Induction of Silent Myocardial Ischemia in Patients with Coronary Artery Disease.* New Eng. J. Med., 318(16): 1005-1012, 1988.

us up for a heart attack by clogging our arteries. Naval pilots fall into three cholesterol categories: Transport pilots tend to have the lowest cholesterols. Land-based fighter pilots, whose job is more dangerous, have higher levels. Carrier-based pilots, who have the riskiest jobs, have the highest levels. Accountants suffer a notorious rise in cholesterol during tax season. FUD can also increase the production of certain "stress chemicals," and can make our platelets more "sticky," raising the odds of a blood clot. It's fear, uncertainty and doubt.

How about FUD and high blood pressure? Although it is often difficult to point to one factor, because many are linked to blood pressure, studies have shown a strong relationship between hypertension and fear, uncertainty and doubt. A 1962 study[2] observed that Zulus who moved into urban environments had higher blood pressure than Zulus who remained in the traditional tribal setting. Two studies reported in the 1970s,[3,4] found that people living in what I call "high FUD" areas, with higher crime rates and more calls for the police and firefighters than other areas, had significantly more hypertension (high blood pressure). "Anticipatory FUD," the fear, uncertainty and doubt we feel as we await a challenge can push our pressure up. Dr. Elliot[5] measured the blood pressure in football players at the University of Nebraska. Their average blood pressure was higher before the game than at half time.

FUD-induced "stress chemicals" can even cause our bodies to secrete less insulin, thus raising the spectre of diabetes, which itself can harm our arteries, among other things. If FUD

---

[2]Gampel B, et al: *Urbanization and hypertension among Zulu adults.* J Chronic Dis 1962; 15:67.

[3] Harburg E., et al. *A family set method for estimating heredity and stress.* I.   A pilot survey of blood pressure among negroes in high and low stress areas, Detroit, 1966-1967. J. Chronic Dis 1970;23:69.

[4]Berkman LF, Syme SL. *Social networks, host resistance, and mortality: a nine-year follow-up study of Alameda County residents.* Am J Epidemiol 1979;1109:186-204

[5]Eliot,R. *The dynamics of hypertension—An overview: Present practices, new possibilities, and new approaches.* Am Heart J 1988:116:583.

is dangerous, the opposite is true. If you try to kill rabbits by feeding them high-cholesterol diets, *but regularly pet and talk to them*, their arteries will not harden as quickly as the arteries of rabbits given the same food, but not the nice attention.

Epidemiologists were amazed a few decades ago when they found a little town in Pennsylvania, called Rosetta, where both the incidence (morbidity) of CAD (coronary artery disease) and death rate (mortality) were very low. Just a few miles up the road, the town of Bangor had the usual high rate of death and disability due to CAD. Why were the people in one town so much healthier than those in the other?

Rosetta had been settled sometime around the turn of the century by stone cutters and their families from Southern Italy. They ate a high-fat diet, which should have made them all candidates for a heart attack. But they took a siesta after a long lunch, they maintained close family ties and loving relationships. They were not money-rich people, but I believe they had meaningful lives. They knew who they were, and how they fit into their community. They knew that they were part of a large, caring group. Like the rabbits, they were getting "petted."

By the 1970s, however, their way of life was changing. The children were going away to school, the strong family ties were weakening. The town was changing: cars made the people mobile, TVs meant the end of the town's relative isolation. Their diets were the same as ever, but now the people of Rosetta found themselves being hit by, and dying from, CAD at a much higher rate.

Living a Life of FUD

Some people may not know that they're living a FUD-filled life. As far as they know, and as far as anyone can tell, they're calm folks with a NICE approach to life. Inside, however, they may be a disaster waiting to happen.

Years ago, I used to hook patients up to biofeedback equipment in my office, the machines helped them learn to relax by monitoring their progress and providing feedback. Dr. Elliot took the idea one step further. He has pioneered the use of biofeedback-like equipment to identify what he calls "Hot Reactors," people who react to a little problem with a lot of internal stress.

The technique is simple: Patients are hooked up to a small machine which measures their cardiovascular performance when they perform various tasks, such as counting backward by sevens from seven hundred, or playing a video game. Counting backward by sevens from seven hundred as rapidly as you can is a bit tricky. And the video game is rigged—you can't win.

Dr. Elliot estimates that about twenty percent of us are "Hot Reactors." Even though we may look calm and cool on the outside, even though we don't seem to care if we win the video game, our body is reacting as if our lives hung in the balance. The internal alarm bells ring so loudly, so insistently, we produce dangerously large amounts of stress chemicals. We're like sports cars with the pedal pushed to the floor, racing across a twisty, bumpy road: Sooner or later we're going to run out of gas, or crash.

"Hot Reactors" are not necessarily the Type A personality we're familiar with—the hard-driving, hostile type that has to get ahead at any cost. "Hot Reactors" may appear to be easy-going types, or they may really be easy-going folks. The point is, behavior does not always reflect what's happening inside the body. And while hotheads may make our lives difficult, "Hot Reactors" may be making their own lives short.

"Hot Reactors" may not feel FUD, but their bodies are *over-reacting* as if they did.

Rats, FUD, and Alice Cooper

Barry and I show a certain slide during our seminars. The left half of the slide shows a picture of normal heart muscle taken from a rat. The heart muscle looks very healthy, as if it were right out of a textbook. The right half of the slide shows a picture of heart muscle taken from a dead rat. It looks terrible; the nice, neat patterns of a healthy heart are distorted.

It seems that a group of rats, with very healthy heart muscle, were put into cages and forced to listen to a recording of a cat chasing rats. Fifteen minutes on, fifteen minutes off, the poor rats heard these terrible sounds. As far as they knew, the cat was right around the corner. As far as they knew, their lives were in immediate danger. Pretty soon, the rats started dying of FUD. There were no cats anywhere near, the rats were never in danger, but they died. And upon autopsy, the researchers found necrosis—death—of the heart muscle.

One night, some fourteen years ago, I came home late, as I often did. My daughter Barbara, who was then twelve years old, said: "Daddy, I want to go see Alice Cooper."

It was late and I was tired, but I felt guilty about not spending more time with her, so I said: "OK, hop in the car and tell me where she lives, I'll take you there."

Barbara looked at me as if I were from Mars. "You're so square, Daddy! Alice Cooper is not a she, he's a he. He's a rock star!"

Well, the next night I found myself at the Forum with Barbara and ten or twelve thousand excited young girls. The place was packed, all the girls were jumping up and down on their chairs, dancing in the aisles as Alice Cooper performed. I had no idea who Alice Cooper was, and was not particularly interested in the music, so I came prepared. I brought ear plugs, a little flashlight and a medical book to read.

About halfway through the concert, Barbara leaned over,

yanked the ear plug out of my right ear and shouted: "Daddy!
You're embarrassing me!"

Do your kids ever say that? I asked her how I was embarrassing her. She said: "You're the only one reading a book!"

I looked to the right, to the left, forward, behind, into the
upper levels. She was right. I was the only one reading a
book.

Again she said: "You're embarrassing me because you're
the only one reading a book. Tomorrow, everybody in school
will be talking about it!"

"All right, what would you like me to do?" I asked. She
insisted that I stand up on my chair and watch the concert. So
I stood up for the rest of the concert, watching the man on
stage cutting the heads off of rubber chickens and otherwise
"performing." I forgot to put my ear plug back in, so the next
morning I had an incredible earache. Not only that, I had a
pounding headache, my back hurt, my neck ached, and I felt
lousy. I wondered: Is Alice Cooper doing to me what the
record did to the rats?

FOUR STEPS TO BEATING FUD

Luckily, we're more complex than rats. We have a greater
ability to interpret and shape our lives. For Grandfather, life
was NICE, it was always a New, Interesting, Challenging
Experience. For some of the engineers, the NICE life of
putting Americans on the moon turned to FUD because they
feared losing their jobs. It's sometimes hard to escape FUD.
As Barry and I write this, for example, we are listening to the
news reports giving what little information is available as the
U.S.-led coalition forces push into Kuwait on Day 1 of the
ground assault. My godson, Lance Corporal Carlos Cueva of
the U.S. Marines, is there. In his last letter, written aboard a

troop ship, Carlos wrote that he and his fellow Marines were waiting to hit the beach. Am I fearful, am I filled with uncertainty and doubt? You bet I am. And, to be honest, there's not a lot I can do to change my feelings. Not now. Not yet.

Fortunately, most situations in life are not as frightening as the prospect of losing a loved one. Still, hot reactors or not, we often fall into FUD. How can we stay in NICE?

#1 – Develop Positive Perception

I believe that the first step toward NICE lies in our perception. You see, the stress that propels us into FUD doesn't have to. What we call "stress" is usually neutral, not necessarily good or bad. Attorneys, for example, often work long hard hours. I have seen many attorneys as patients, and know many socially. (My eldest and fourth sons, Howard and Steven, are attorneys.) Some attorneys look upon their tremendous work load as a challenge, a chance to do some good, to prove themselves, and to get ahead. Others see the same work as an incredible burden. The same stress (lots of work) can be NICE or FUD, depending on how you look at it. It's a matter of perception.

I see this again and again with patients complaining of stress-related stomach problems, headaches, neck and back pains and other symptoms. Imagine two clerks in the same office, doing pretty much the same work. One clerk thinks the work is below his talents, resents taking orders from a woman-boss, and believes that he could have been rich if only his parents had given him the money for law school. The other clerk, the child of immigrants, is glad to have a job that pays her enough to go to night school, where she's completing her college degree. The two clerks are doing the same work, receiving the same pay, and taking orders from the same boss.

For the first clerk, work is dreadful. For the other, it's a great opportunity to get ahead. It's a matter of perception.

I had a patient, a 53-year old man named Fred, whose job as a construction foreman was very NICE. Then the owners told Fred that they wanted him to cut costs by using cheaper materials and, in general, doing a shoddy job. They ordered him to cut costs by twenty percent—or else. This was a terrible blow for Fred, who took great pride in his work. FUD hit him like a sledge hammer, sending him to my office with a long-list of complaints. He quit the job rather than lowering his standards, but his replacement had no trouble doing a shoddy job. The point is not that Fred was better than the other guy, but that what was FUD for Fred was NICE for someone else. It's a matter of perception. That's why I believe that changing our perception is the first step toward turning FUD into NICE.

Positive perception allows us to control our world by changing our interpretation of everything that happens. From the smallest event to the most monumental, our world is largely a picture painted by our perception. I believe that positive perception is what makes many of our dreams come true. I also believe that dreaming, and the ability to dream new dreams, is a vital part of positive perception.

Many of us endure terrible hardships: Positive perception helps us through the difficult days. Many of us believe that we are failures: Positive perception helps us focus on our success. In so doing, positive perception can strengthen our hand against the tasks ahead.

How do we develop positive perception? By dreaming of the great things we can do, especially those we can do for others. By keeping our eyes fixed firmly on our successes, those in our past, and those we know are in our future. By believing in ourselves, no matter what the circumstances, no matter what others may say. By taking control of our lives, even if only in our minds.

How do we change our perception? That's the subject of this book, and a lot of thought and effort. One of the efforts we can make is to become part of something great, something wonderful.

#2 – Dream the Impossible Dream

Life was always NICE for Grandfather. It didn't matter what was going wrong, and there was always something going wrong. He never had much money. He was forced to bear the same slights and indignities we all do. Yet his life was always NICE, because he felt he was spearheading the crusade to feed and clothe the poor, to raise money for their doctors and for their education. How could he be uncertain when he knew that the food he distributed helped keep poor people alive? Where was there room for doubt when he knew that the money he raised paid for the operation that saved the child's life? And how could he feel lonely and isolated when everyone in the community knew and respected him?

Yes, unhappy things happened to him. But all the NICE he had built up in his life—in his mind—was a shield. So strongly was his perception focused on the good things in life, most of the FUD just bounced off and disappeared.

One of the best ways to change our perception is to go on a crusade, a holy crusade to right wrongs. We should crusade, not for our sake, but for the sake of others. Go back to that list you made at the end of Chapter 3. Pick one of those dreams and make it come true for someone else. Years ago I was at Reverend Dan Morgan's church in Los Angeles. I can still picture that powerful preacher as he stood on the pulpit and thundered: "I don't want a great power to use, I want a great power to use me!"

Let's be used. Let's use our talents to help others. At the

same time, we'll fill our lives with NICE as a protection against the inevitable FUD that occasionally comes our way. I recently read that comedian Danny Thomas of TV's "Make Room For Daddy" died. He made lots of money, but early in his career, during the Depression things didn't look good. When things looked as if they were as low as they could possibly go, he prayed to St. Jude, the patron saint of hopeless causes. He asked St. Jude to help him find a way so he could build a shrine. That shrine, his crusade, became St. Jude's Children's Hospital in Memphis, Tennessee. That shrine, his crusade, saved many young lives. Great crusades like that make life very NICE.

Giving is a great way to make yourself feel as if you belong, like Grandfather. Give unconditionally, without asking for anything in return. But don't worry, you'll get back plenty. Let's be used. Let's be like Grandfather, like Rev. Morgan, like Danny Thomas, like Albert Schweitzer, like Mother Teresa. Let's feed people, let's clothe them, let's teach them, let's help them smile, let's change laws that need changing, let's take on impossible challenges, let's right unrightable wrongs. Let's do so much for others. There's no way our lives can be anything but NICE.

#3 – Forgive Them

Retired General Benjamin O. Davis, Jr. lead World War II's 332nd Fighter Group, the first group of black pilots in the then-segregated U.S. armed forces. Most of the 332nd flyers won the Distinguished Flying Cross, and proved that black pilots are every bit as good as white flyers. By the end of the war, the 332nd had knocked out some three hundred enemy planes while flying over three thousand missions over Europe. In 1932 General Davis became the only black cadet at West

Point. His presence at the all-white military academy back in the 1930s made a lot of people unhappy. In fact, the other cadets gave him the silent treatment and refused to speak to him for the entire first year. Rather than responding to their cruel bigotry with anger, as many would have done, he looked at them with pity. Rather than remaining in FUD for four long years, he kept his life NICE by selecting his perception.

Let's take a lesson from the fighting general. When someone does us wrong, let's forgive them. Let's imagine that they're children and that they can't help themselves. Let's pity them because their perceptions are so limited. Let's ignore them. Let's discount our grievance immediately, before it turns to FUD.

#4 – Don't Sweat It

Finally, when FUD-like things do happen, as they occasionally will, don't get upset. There are three cardinal rules we should follow if we want to live a long, FUD-free life. I don't know who made these rules up. Whoever it was, they were pretty wise.

1. **Don't sweat the little things in life.**

2. **Everything is little.**

3. **If you can't flee, flow.**

Develop positive perception, dream the impossible dream, forgive them, and don't sweat it: Four steps for beating FUD.

R$_x$: TOGETHER

It's easy to fall victim to FUD. Three days into the land war against Iraq, I still wasn't able to stop worrying about my young godson over there. I consider myself to be a very positive man, yet I can't completely shut the door against my fears. When my daughter died, I was beset by doubts. How could I, the great doctor who saved so many lives, allow my own little girl to die? What was wrong with me?

Now and then, it's my connection with others that pulls me back, that gently turns my eyes toward the NICE parts of life. I believe that being part of a community is a powerful medicine. Whether the community is a family, a neighborhood, a church or a synagogue, or any other sharing and caring group, feeling that you belong is medicinal. I feel that I am part of my immediate family, and my extended family back in Philadelphia. I feel that I'm still a part of my old neighborhood, still a part of the people, those who are living and those who have passed on. (I don't feel that I am a part of my present neighborhood, but that's primarily my fault.) I feel that I am a part of the medical community, a part of my circle of friends, a part of my family of co-religionists. I feel that I'm a part of our great democracy.

To continually remind myself that I am part of many communities, I often rip a regular-sized piece of paper into several smaller pieces, which I scatter on my desk. I look at the pieces, one here, one there, another way over there. They're isolated and unconnected. Then I move the pieces back together. Each piece is still separate, an individual, yet it touches the others, drawing from them, contributing to their effort to form a full sheet of paper—a community. Without losing its identity, each little piece becomes part of the whole. Each piece strengthens, and draws strength, from the others. As I look at this, I say to myself:

Joyful are those who dwell in peace,
Peaceful are those who dwell in love,
Loving are those who dwell in forgiveness,
Forgiving are those who dwell in understanding,
Understanding are those who dwell in wisdom,
Wise are those who dwell in wisdom,
Wise are those who dwell in joy.

Not everybody with FUD is isolated from their community, and not every member of a community is living an always-NICE life. Still, I believe that belonging, being a part of something, and giving yourself wholeheartedly to your community, is a wonderful medicine.

Positive thoughts are strengthened by positive actions, and positive actions prompt positive thoughts. Putting together the pieces of the paper remind us that strong as we are, individual as we are, we take on a new form and new power when we are with others. Especially when we do for others.

"Together" is a wonderful word. Let's turn the word into action by helping others. My son Steven, an attorney, spends every Friday afternoon giving free legal advice at a senior citizen's center. He's using his specialized knowledge to help others. My banker fingerpaints with emotionally disturbed young children, and takes others out on outings to ballgames and shows. She gives her love and her time. Whether you donate your knowledge or your love, you are working together with someone.

Together, Grandfather and I became a doctor. Together, you and some eager young child can be a doctor, a lawyer, a teacher. Together, you and a troubled youngster can smile for the first time. Together, you and a homeless person can build a new life. Together, you and a frightened runaway can find peace. Together, you and a forgotten oldster can learn to love life again. *Together:* It's a medicinal word. It's a magical word.

CHAPTER FIVE

THE GOAL IS JOY

"He that is of a merry heart hath a continual feast."
—Proverbs 15:15

It was a beautiful sunny day at Roxbury Park in Beverly Hills. I had come to see my son Steven and the soccer team he coached. Watching the game on the field was fun—little boys running back and forth, trying to kick the ball into the goals. However, the game on the sidelines was much more interesting:

"Foul! Foul!" screamed Smith, one of the little boy's parents, at the referee.

"How could you let him get past you?" Jones bellowed at his son. "Next time go to the side, go to the side!"

"Uh, excuse me, sir," Steven said. "Let me do the coaching."

"Shut up!" snapped Smith.

"You call yourself a coach!" sneered Jones. "Look, look! The other team just scored another goal, and it's *all your fault!*"

"Why is it the coach's fault?" I asked. They didn't know that I was Steven's father.

"Because this jerk of a coach lets the bad players play," snapped Jones. "And when you put the bad players on the field, you lose. That's why!"

By now all the parents had become involved. Steven tried to explain his coaching philosophy: "I want all the boys to have fun and learn how to go play soccer. Even the less-skilled boys should have a chance. You can't learn to play, and you can't have fun, if you sit on the bench. Besides, if we're having fun, who cares if we lose?"

"Who cares if we lose? We care if we lose?" the parents screamed over and over. The scream began to sound like a terrifying war cry as the angry mothers and fathers advanced on Steven.

"You're ruining my son's life by not teaching him to win, win, WIN!" exclaimed Jones.

"You ought to bench the bad players," said Smith.

"But your son is the worst player on the team," Steven protested.

"That's right. And he'd rather sit on the bench for a winning team than play for a bad one," asserted Smith.

"Win! Win! Win!" was the parent's chant. I pushed my way through the crowd to my son's side, but did not reveal who I was.

"Why worry about winning?" Steven asked in self-defense.

"Why worry about winning?" the parents screamed in disbelief. "Why worry about winning!?"

"Yeah. The point is to have fun."

"Fun?" the parents roared, unable to believe what they were hearing. "Fun? Fun?"

I thought it was time to speak in Steven's defense. Before I could say a word, however, an elderly man, beautifully attired in a gray pin-striped suit, carrying an umbrella and homburg, drew me away.

"Pardon me Dr. Fox," he said. "I know what you're going to say. Please reconsider."

"But Steven is right. Having fun is more important that winning."

"I agree," replied the elderly gentleman, a twinkle in his eye. "I agree. But consider this. Our economy, our society, our entire way of life depends upon what happens on playing fields such as this all over America. Look at that little boy over there. He's one of the worst on the team. On any other team he would sit on the bench. But Steven allows him to play. The little boy loves to play. He always has a good time, and he does not care who wins. He is a happy, easygoing child, just as his parents are happy, easygoing adults."

"What has that to do with anything?" I asked, impatient to get back to Steven's defense.

"Have patience, Dr. Fox," the elderly man said, mirth dancing on his every word. "Look at Jones' son. He is certainly the best player on the team. He has, however, an unfortunate tendency to scream at his opponents, to insult the referee, and belittle his teammates. He trips and fouls his opponents when the referee is not looking. He kicks himself when he commits an error. He excoriates his teammates when they goof. In short, he is a miserable, ill-adjusted child, just as his parents are miserable, ill-adjusted adults."

"That's awful," I protested. "Look at his parents. They're abrasive and unhappy, they've been divorced a couple times each, their blood pressure is sky-high, they take all kinds of pills, they stuff themselves with food to try to forget their misery. They both have ulcers now, and they're sure to have heart attacks before they're fifty!"

"Yes! Indeed!" the elderly man practically shouted, hopping from one foot to the other. "Indubitably! Most indubitably!"

"Why are you so happy?" I asked, sure that this guy was crazy.

"I am happy because the miserable little boy is growing up just like his miserable parents."

"That's terrible!"

"No," he chortled, jumping up and down. "That's what makes our country great!"

Now I knew I had a nut on my hands. He stopped to catch

his breath before continuing: "That happy little boy is going to grow up well-adjusted, just like his parents. In short, he is going to be a parasitic, unproductive threat to the American way of life.

"That unhappy boy, by contrast," he continued, "is going to grow up as unhappy as his parents are. He will most certainly require psychologists and psychiatrists, lawyers to handle his divorces and lawsuits, doctors for his high blood pressure and heart problems, radio talk show hosts to call in to, and accountants to count all the money he will make."

"But that's depressing," I said.

"No! It's wonderful," the elderly man giggled with undisguised glee. "You've seen the doctor's, the attorney's, the psychologist's offices here in Beverly Hills, and next door in Century City. You know how expensive they are to maintain. The rent on those beautiful offices is high, the beautiful furniture costs a fortune. When you add the cost of expense accounts, fancy cars and vacations, you realize that it requires a great deal of money to support all these doctors, attorneys, psychologists and the like."

"What has that got to do with children's sports?" I cried out in frustration.

"Children's sports are a vital part of the process, a vital link in the chain. If these young boys are not taught that winning is all that counts; if these young boys do not learn that there is no room for sportsmanship and fun; if these young boys do not learn that it does not matter who you step on as long as you get to the top; if these young boys do not learn these lessons, they simply will not grow up to be as unhappy and unhealthy as their parents are. And if they are not miserable and sick, they will not spend a fortune on doctors, psychologists, attorneys, alcohol, drugs and pills. They will not waste small fortunes buying things they do not need in a futile attempt to purchase happiness. They will not spend billions overeating. They will not buy fancy cars to impress others. They will not spend obscene amounts of money at the in-spots just so they can be seen. Why, if everyone grew up happy, our entire economy would absolutely collapse! Our society would be destroyed!"

I had to admit, there was a certain logic to what he was saying.

"What better way to ensure the unhappiness of children than to take a simple, pleasurable activity like kicking a ball around a field, and ruin it by having parents scream at the children from the sidelines? It is masterful, masterful! It puts tremendous pressure on the poor boys," he squealed with delight.

"What better place to start making them miserable," I said, "and to start boosting the economy, than on the playing field?"

"Yes! Yes!" the elderly man was practically dancing with joy.

"So you're saying that children's sports are a national priority?" I asked.

"Exactly. Without little leagues such as this, our great country would perish. Good day, Dr. Fox."

With that, he placed his homburg on his head and strolled slowly off. There was a certain logic to what he had said. I was about to join the parents screaming "WIN, WIN, WIN!" but thought better of it.

You see, the real goal in life is joy. The goal is always joy.

IS JOY A PAIN?

"Gladness of heart is the life of a man, and the
rejoicing of a man is length of days."
—Ecclesiasticus 30:22

About a year ago, Barry wrote a wonderful pamphlet on joy, which he called "Six Tips For Being Joyful." I showed it to a doctor I know. Let's call him Dr. Smith. When Dr. Smith read the pamphlet, his face turned purple, the veins on his forehead stood out, his hands shook with rage. "How can you believe in this stuff!" he shouted at me. "This is phony-baloney crap, not medicine! This hurts people!"

"Hurts people?" I asked. "How can joy hurt anyone?"

"Don't you see what you're doing?" he snarled. "You're telling them to believe in things that aren't real! Ulcers are real! Cancer is real! Heart attacks are real! Medicine is real! Joy is not real—it's crap! I'll take reality over joy any day."

I loved his reaction! I was so excited, I immediately grabbed the phone and called Barry. "Smith hates it!" I shouted.

"Great!" Barry exclaimed. "Now we *know* it's good."

Barry and I laughed about this, for we often use the nonsense, "reality-loving" Dr. Smith as the litmus test of our writing. If he doesn't like it, we know it's good.

Like Dr. Smith, many people refuse to be happy, treat laughter as the enemy, take offense at joy. One of my patients was a fifty-three year old bank president named Jake, who proudly called himself the "acid in my employee's lives."

"I don't *have* stress," he told Barry and me. "I *give* stress." Jake, who had been raised in an orphanage, relished making life miserable for his employees. You could tell something was wrong as soon as you stepped into his bank. The secretaries, clerks, and loan officers rarely looked up from their desks, busying themselves with real or imaginary work. When they had to get something, they darted quickly about the bank, heads buried in their papers. Barry described them as "mice afraid to be noticed by the cat."

Employees, who had the misfortune of making a minor mistake, were hit with a withering storm of Jake's sarcasm.

They were ridiculed in front of everyone, including customers and their fellow employees. When Barry asked Jake what he thought about joy, the banker laughed and said:

"Joy? Sure, I'm a joyful guy. I like to start each day with a smile and get it over with quick. Being happy all the time just means you're fooling yourself." He rose from his chair, pounding a fist on the desk as he snarled: "It's my duty in life to make people stop deceiving themselves!"

Like Jake, many people believe it's their duty to let you know just how miserable you really are. They seem to delight in destroying your joy. Of course, the anger they hurl at you is fueled by rage they have within. They have no choice but to try to "teach you a lesson," because they feel so miserable. They rip you apart because they feel so very inadequate.

Hostility Hurts. . .

It hurts you as much as it hurts them. For example, the February, 1991 issue of *Medical Aspects of Human Sexuality* reports on a study conducted by Redford Williams of Duke University. Back in the 1960s, Williams and Ilene Siegler examined the results of personality tests given to 830 University of North Carolina students. Twenty years later, they compared the blood tests of those students to their personality tests. The young people who scored high on hostility scales became adults with high total cholesterols, and low amounts of the "good" cholesterol (HDL, or high-density lipoprotein). What's the connection between hostility and high cholesterol? We can't describe the exact mechanisms, but it seems likely that anger triggers the release of stress hormones. These hormones, in turn, cause the body to release fat into the bloodstream, prompting other reactions which lead to the elevated cholesterol.

Being angry now and then won't clog your arteries. But persistent, long-term anger may put you in line for a heart attack.

THE TEN-DROP GIRL

When Barry and I sat down to discuss what would go into this chapter, he said that we must include the story of the "Ten Drop Woman." As soon as he told me the story, I agreed.

Barry met the "Ten Drop Girl," whose name is Patty, at a seminar he gave here in Los Angeles. She spoke with him after the presentation, after he had answered all the remaining questions, shook everyone's hand, and autographed books. A beautiful woman in her early thirties, she walked with a bounce in her step and radiated joy. Even her whisky, Lauren Bacall-like voice was lively and joyful. Her story, however, was bittersweet.

Patty has no memories of her parents; they were killed in the auto accident that left her with a shattered leg. After several surgeries and several years in an orphanage, she was put into the foster-child program, and went to live with a foster-family. "The first family was nice," she said, "although they made a point of telling everyone that I was their *foster-daughter.*" Patty was with them for only six months before being sent back to the orphanage. She never found out why they sent her back.

The young girl stayed with several more families, some for a few months, one for a little over a year, bouncing between foster-home and the orphanage. Some of the families were nice, she said, others neglected her. One was outright abusive, she was beaten and even, once, sexually abused. Finally, she settled down with the Thompsons. "They were in their late forties. My social worker thought they were old to take in a twelve-year old girl. I'm glad they did."

The Thompsons were the only ones who introduced Patty as "our daughter" (not "foster-daughter," or "the girl we're taking care of"). For the first time she could remember, Patty said, she felt loved. The Thompsons didn't have much money, in fact, they were the poorest of her foster-families. "But they were my first, my only family," she said.

"The day I arrived there, my social worker dropped me off. They had a party for me, Mom, Dad and Melissa, my new sister, with a cake and presents. I got two dresses, a make-up kit and a bicycle. That was the most birthday presents I had ever been given, and it wasn't even my birthday. And the bike was used, it wasn't my size, but I loved it. It was the first bike I ever owned. I cried."

After the party Melissa Thompson, three years older than Patty, took the shy orphan-girl around the neighborhood, introducing her to her friends, chatting about make-up, boys, and other things. Patty was stunned—she had never been treated so well, had never been welcomed with arms so open. It was like being in fantasy-land.

That night, when Patty sat down with her new family for dinner, her father led them in a little ceremony. Lifting his water glass high, he said: *"Our cup of life is filled with joy."* Then, setting the glass back on the table, he removed one drop of water with his spoon. Letting that drop fall to the table, he said: *"I remove today's anger."* Taking another drop from his glass, letting it fall to the table, he continued: *"I remove today's fear."* Drop by drop, he eliminated ten negatives from his cup of life.

"Then, after he removed the 'ten plagues' from our cup of life," Patty explained, "he refilled the glass and said:

A drop of love,
A drop of warmth,

> *A drop of friendship,*
> *A drop of song,*
> *A drop of laughter,*
> *A drop of learning,*
> *A drop of growing,*
> *A drop of sharing,*
> *A drop of helping,*
> *A drop of forgiving.*
> *Ten drops make an ocean of joy.*

"He gave the glass to Mom. She said 'Ten drops make an ocean of joy' and took a sip. Melissa did the same, then gave the glass to me. Just for a second I was angry, I was furious. I thought, what do these people know about suffering. I know about suffering! I'm an orphan, I've been kicked around. I've been beaten and sexually abused. What do they know about suffering? Then I thought, but what do I know about joy? So I said, 'Ten drops make an ocean of joy,' and took a sip."

Patty told Barry how ten little drops really did turn into an ocean of joy in her life. The drops of love, warmth, friendship, song, laughter, learning, growing, sharing, helping and forgiving she shared with her new family washed away her sorrows. "For the first time, I was really joyful," she said. "Not that I was really depressed before. I was sad sometimes and happy sometimes. But now I was really joyful."

Three joyful years sped by before Mr. Thompson died of a sudden heart attack. Mrs. Thompson, who had little money, fought to keep Patty. The authorities, however, decided the now-fifteen year old would be better off in the orphanage. Mrs. Thompson, the only woman Patty ever called "Mom," had to move across country to be close to her family and Melissa went off to college.

"Going back to the orphanage was like having your smile ripped off, and tears glued on forever. I cried for weeks. Then

I started doing the ten drops. I was embarrassed; I didn't want anyone to see. They found out, of course, and they called me the 'Ten Drop Girl'. You know what? It made a big difference. I saw every drop of bad I took out of my cup as a tear, and every drop of joy going in as a smile. Ten tears out, ten smiles in. It works."

That's the formula: Ten tears out, ten smiles in.

Good things and bad things drop into our lives. Some of the goods are great; some of the bads are terribly painful. A lot of us—too many of us—are experts on suffering. We know all about sadness, and we can describe misery in every little detail. But what do we know of joy?

If it seems that life is a school of sorrow, that's only because our curriculum is all wrong. We can know as much about joy as we do about sorrow. We can teach ourselves, and each other, to drink the drops of good, to let them wash away the bad. And what are these ten drops? They're not piles of money, they're not mansions or fancy cars, they're simple little things like laughter and friendship. A drop of song, a drop of sharing. Ten tears out, ten smiles in.

"Melissa and I are practically neighbors now," Patty told Barry. "Our kids go to school together. Mom died three years ago. At the service, we took ten drops out of the glass, and put ten drops back in. Everyone took a sip from the glass. We poured the rest onto the dirt piled over her."

She's lost two sets of parents, many surgeries were required to fix her leg, she was kicked around from foster-home to foster-home, she was treated as the "kid we're taking care of," she was physically and sexually abused. She found a wonderful new family, she went to a topnotch college, she married, she has two children and a close relationship with her sister. It's ten tears out, ten smiles in for Patty. "That's the formula for joy."

WORRY, THE ENEMY OF JOY

"We consume our tomorrows fretting about our yesterdays."

—Persius

Why aren't we nearly as joyful as we could be—as we should be? Why do we seem to focus on the tears—ignoring the smiles? I hear many answers to this question:

- *"Who can have fun with the economy going to pot?"*
- *"I'm too frightened right now by street crime to be happy."*
- *"I've got too many responsibilities."*
- *"My job's weighing me down."*
- *"Kids have time for fun, I've got to think about serious things."*
- *"My marriage just fell apart. What's there to smile about?"*

Fear, a recent hurt, too much responsibility, overwork—there are plenty of reasons for not being joyful. Some of them are good reasons—it is difficult to be joyful when a loved one has died, for example. But if you dig past many of the reasons for not being joyful, if you dig to the very bottom, you'll hit the real reason: Worry. We all worry that we're not good enough, not strong enough, not smart enough, not fast enough, not tough enough. We worry that we won't get ahead. We worry that we're going to fail. We worry that someone's going to laugh at us. We worry that we'll lose our money, our status, our "face." We worry ourselves out of doing things. We worry ourselves into doing nothing. We worry ourselves into fear. We worry ourselves into shying away from love. We worry ourselves away from joy.

Worry is brilliant: It tells us that we can't be happy, so we had better spend our lives finding fault with others. Worry is afraid we'll try something new and fail, so it tells us that the "something new" is not important. Worry tells us that we're too busy, that we absolutely *must* watch those great new shows on TV. Worry sits us in front of the television set for hours at a time, because you can't "fail" watching television. TV keeps us busy, so we "haven't time" for anything else, something that might challenge us, something we might fail at. Worry tells us that we have to learn to do one thing right before we try something new, but since we're never going to learn the first thing, we better forget about the second. Might as well watch TV.

Worry is the #1 stopper in our lives. Worry is the main reason we don't do things—we don't dare. Worry is the enemy of effort and imagination. Worry saps our talents. Worry tells us that we can't do it. Worry tears away at our belief in ourselves. Worry strangles our lives. Is it any wonder that worry is the enemy of joy?

TOO WORRIED TO LIVE

> *"Worms eat you when you're dead;*
> *worries eat you up when you're alive."*
> — Yiddish Proverb

I was once asked to go to the hospital and see a man named Tim. Plagued with asthma for decades, this thirty-eight year old, unmarried man was laboring to breathe through a fat plastic tube taped into his mouth. I could hear the sounds of the machine "breathing" strong and steady, those characteristic sounds I wouldn't know how to put in print. And I could imagine the air swirling through passageways in Tim's lungs, through the branches and sub-branches of his airways that only hours before were being squeezed shut by muscles that seemed intent on keeping all air out.

"Tim worries about everything," his brother told me one

day at the hospital. "His IQ is 130, but he's got a little job with
an adding machine. They won't promote him unless he takes
a test he could pass in his sleep, but he's afraid to take it. Once
he actually signed up, but the morning of the test he had an
asthma attack. They had to rush him to the hospital and shoot
him full of adrenaline to keep him breathing. Our parents
used to try to get him to do things when we were kids, but he'd
panic and have an asthma attack.

His brother told me that Tim won't date because he's
worried about "striking out." Tim wanted to take a beginning
rock climbing class with his brother, but began wheezing as
soon as they got to the rocks. That was the end of that. Tim
joined a Toastmaster's club to learn how to speak. He's been
in it for a year, but hasn't given a single speech yet. He gets
sick every time it's his turn to give a speech.

Tim's worry was literally strangling him. He worried
about failing tests. He worried that he wouldn't impress
women. He worried he'd give a bad speech. He worried about
everything.

After the breathing tube had been removed, I spoke with
Tim. He was obviously a very intelligent fellow. His knowledge of American and British history was astonishing. "Since
you love history so much," I asked, "why aren't you teaching
history?"

"You need a credential to teach high school," he replied.

"How about teaching at a university?" I suggested.

"Well, professors have to serve on committees and put up
with all kinds of bureaucratic nonsense," he quickly replied.

"OK. How about writing some books and sharing your
knowledge?"

"The publishers would want me to write a commercial
book, but I don't want to pander to public taste," he answered.
When I suggested he publish the book himself, he argued that
he would have to spend too much time dealing with the busi-

ness aspects of publishing, so he wouldn't be a historian any more.

Then I said: "You're obviously a bright man. Why haven't you moved up at work in all these years?"

Tim pointed out that if he were promoted, he'd have more responsibility. And if he had more responsibility, he'd have to work longer hours. And if he worked longer hours, he would no longer have his evenings and weekends free for his study.

"How about a wife, a family?" I continued.

"What woman would want me?" he asked. "I'm thirty-eight years old. I've got no money and no real future."

"But you could make money—make a future!" I exclaimed. "With your brains, you could be rich."

"Yes, but I don't want a woman who's only interested in me because of my money," he replied. "Besides, having a family would take time away from my studies."

No matter what I said, Tim had a reason for not doing anything but burying his life in a book. Don't get me wrong; learning simply for the sake of knowing is one of the greatest pleasures in life. But I believe that Tim was really motivated by his fear of failing as a professor, as an author, as a husband or father, as anything. As I read his medical history, and interviewed his brother and parents, it became clear that Tim was simply too worried to face most of life. He hid in his safe job, and in a hobby that allowed him to shut out the world. When challenged, Tim's fear was transformed into asthma.

Interestingly enough, getting sick took care of Tim's problems. Being sick gave him a "valid" reason to worry. His asthma turned him into a victim—a man with a terrible disease who received attention and plenty of sympathy. I don't know what happened to Tim, but I suspect he's still huddled on his little piece of life, eyes firmly glued to his books, strangling himself. Worry wouldn't let Tim do anything. Worry certainly wouldn't let Tim be happy.

"ANWYRGAN" (an-ree-gan)

"Worry gives a small thing a big shadow."
—Swedish proverb

Our word "worry" comes from Latin "wyrgan" (ree-gan), meaning "to strangle." That's what we do when we worry: we strangle ourselves, our creativity, our ability to think, our strength, our flexibility, our belief in ourselves, our immune system, our health.

"Joy," on the other hand, comes to us from the Latin word for "jewel." Worry versus joy. Strangulation versus the jewel: the jewel of joy, of life, health and happiness.

Since worry (wyrgan) strangles us, we want to be *anwyrgan* (an-ree-gan). "An" means "without." To be *anwyrgan* means to go through life without strangling ourselves with worry. Let's go through life as jewels of joy.

6 REASONS NOT TO WORRY

"Let us be of good cheer, remembering that misfortunes hardest to bear are those which never come."
—James Russell Lowell

A business man once challenged us at a seminar. He said: "I run a multi-million dollar company. Decisions have to be made every day. A thousand things can go wrong with the product, the sales, the distribution, the advertising, the accounting, the marketing. If I don't worry, who will?"

If you don't worry, who will? Hopefully nobody will. Let's all do what has to be done without strangling ourselves, without staunching the flow of thought, creativity, energy and enthusiasm. Some people believe that worry is valuable, that it somehow helps us. Concern, the realization that there is a problem and the desire to do something about it, is valuable and necessary. Worry, however, chokes us to death. There is no good reason for excessive worry. In fact, here are 6 Great Reasons Not to Worry.

1. Worry Stands in the Way of Positive Action

From birth to death, we're bombarded by negative messages: *"You can't do it." "You can't do it." "You're not good enough." "You'll never make it." "You're going to fail."* These messages, intentional or unintentional, verbal or otherwise, undermine our confidence, sap our energy, and throttle our creativity.

Our brains should get all kinds of messages: Facts, positive feedback, encouragement, discouragement, you can do this, you need more practice before doing that, do this now, do that later. By mixing together all the information, we make our decisions.

When we worry, our mental eye is fixed only on the negative. The positive, encouraging information is always there, but worry does not allow us to see it, hear it, believe it. Worry fixes our mental eye on the negatives, on the images of failure, weakness, or embarrassment. Over and over again, worry consistently shoves the same message to the forefront of our minds. When we should be thinking about the ten thousand things we're going to do, worry tells us we can only do one thing: Fail.

Worry paralyzes us. It stands in the way of our positive thoughts and our positive actions.

2. Worry Destroys Joy—and Health

The human mind cannot entertain two opposing thoughts

for very long. One inevitably displaces the other. We cannot be joyful when we are worried. Neither can we worry when we are joyful. Although joy is a strong emotion, a great emotion, it can be swept aside by worry.

The brain is the largest gland in the body, producing a constant stream of biosubstances which affect every cell in the body. Every thought in our heads affects our biochemistry for better or worse. Thus, a mind constantly full of worry can flood our bodies with worrisome substances, with high-voltage chemicals such as adrenaline and cortisone that, when present in the wrong amounts, at the wrong times, undermine our health.

Worry harms our immune system. Chronic worry reduces the effectiveness of our killer T-cells and other immune system cells. Worry causes heart disease, cancer, stroke, high blood pressure and other killers.

Worry raises our blood cholesterol. A rise in serum cholesterol can be measured as soon as two hours after stress is applied. Unlike catecholamines (adrenaline-like substances) and cortisone, which drop off fairly rapidly after stress, cholesterol remains high for some time. If we look at academic stress, we see that the cholesterol levels remain high even weeks after major examinations in medical school.[1] Researchers examining forty-some studies found that in most studies, stress pushed cholesterol levels up anywhere from 8 to 36%. In some cases of law students studying for the Bar Exam, cholesterol shot up from 150 to 300, some jumping from 250 to 500. I have seen large drops in the HDL (the "good" cholesterol you want) with stress.

If I were some malevolent power who wanted to torture the human race, I wouldn't rely on hurricanes, earthquakes or floods. Instead, I would create a worry virus. A virulent virus,

[1] Dimsdale, J & Herd, JA: Variability of Plasma Lipids in Response to Emotional Arousal. Psychosomatic Med., 44:413-430, 1982.
Francis, K.: Psychologic Correlates of Serum Indicators of Stress in Man: A longitudinal Study. Psychosomatic Med., 41: 617-628, 1976.

it would spread easily, leaping from person to person without physical contact. The worry virus would be worse than natural disasters because worry infection is slow torture, and a lifetime of fears, doubts, and frustrations. The worry virus would turn people's biochemistry upside down, slowly weakening their immune system, sapping their energy, and destroying their creativity.

Worry destroys joy, and our health. But we can shut the door to worry by filling our minds with joy, love, belief in ourselves and other great thoughts.

3. *Worry is a Master Addiction*

Worry is an addiction—one as bad as our addictions to nicotine, alcohol, overeating, and cocaine. Worry, which often leads to other addictions, is the "master addiction."

We are harmed psychologically, physiologically, and socio-logically by worry. It lays us low. We attempt to relieve the terrible feelings by smoking or eating, or with alcohol or drugs. We self-medicate. We ruin our health. But the worry is still there. We grasp for material objects, money and houses and cars and stereos, to alleviate our worry; we need more and more things. But the worry is still there. We take uppers to mask the worry, then we need downers to bring us down. But the worry is still there, along with our new addictions. Millions are caught in this vicious cycle, trapped in a web of addictions, started by the master addiction: worry.

4. *Worry Makes Us Fat—or Starves Us*

Our weight can be strongly related to worry. Many people worry themselves into eating too much. They start young, believing that they're already fat. And because they're fat, they won't have a good boyfriend/girlfriend, they won't get a good job, they won't have this and that. Pretty soon they're convinced they're losers. Now they have a lot to worry about. Those who try to lose weight worry that it won't stay off. They unknowingly sabotage their own diets—and the rest of their lives—through worry. Those who don't try to lose weight worry that they're weak. Worry pushes others the other way—worrying themselves into anorexia or bulimia.

5. We Worry for the Wrong Reasons

We're often less worried about what's happening than we are about what others will say. Losing the big account, for example, is bad. But how many parents take excessive pride in their children's achievements? What happens when their children can't, or won't, measure up? We parents naturally want our children to do well, but how much of our worry is really for ourselves, not our children?

We're rarely worried for the reason we think we are. The weekend warriors at the parks who are so anxious to win: Is victory so important, or are they just really worried about looking bad?

6. Worry Does Not Work

The best argument against worry is that worry does not work. Worry doesn't solve anything; it *creates* problems. Concern—an awareness of problems, a desire to fix them—spurs us on. Concern can help us figure out ways to overcome our difficulties. Worry, on the other hand, paralyzes us. Worry freezes the gears of our mind. Worry simply doesn't work.

Thomas Edison failed many more times than he succeeded. Babe Ruth had more strike outs than home runs. Christopher Columbus, Charles Lindberg and Neil

Armstrong, the first man on the moon, had every reason to worry. David Ben Gurion, the first prime minister of Israel, faced insurmountable odds, yet he went ahead. Solidarity's Lech Walensa took on impossible odds. How much could these people have accomplished if they spent their lives worrying instead of doing?

Worry diminishes us in our own minds. Worry makes our opponents stronger and our troubles larger. Worry saps our belief. Worry prevents positive thoughts and positive action.

R$_x$: DROPS OF JOY

> *"This makes me so sore it gets my dandruff up."*
> —Samuel Goldwyn (of MGM)

Let's borrow Patty's formula for joy: Ten tears out, ten smiles in. Fill a glass with water, almost to the top. Lift your water glass high, say: *"My cup of life is filled with joy."* Set the glass down. Using a spoon, or your finger, take ten drop from the glass, letting each drop fall to the table as you say:

I remove today's anger, fear, self-pity, doubt, jealousy, worry, sadness, unforgiveness, selfishness, and hard-heartedness. I remove all the tears from my life.

Having removed the ten tears from your life, replace them with the ten drops that will become your ocean of joy. Refill your glass as you say:

A drop of love,
A drop of warmth,
A drop of friendship,
A drop of song,

> *A drop of laughter,*
> *A drop of learning,*
> *A drop of growing,*
> *A drop of sharing,*
> *A drop of helping,*
> *A drop of forgiving.*
> *Ten drops make an ocean of joy.*

As you sip from the glass remember that while worries sometimes seem as plentiful as sand on the beach, joy is only ten drops away.

CRUSADE FOR JOY

> *"The best way to cheer yourself up is*
> *to try to cheer somebody else up."*
> —Mark Twain

The best way to rid ourselves of worry is to take action! There's the symbolic, inward "ten drop" action. As for outward action, get on a crusade for joy. As long as one person is sad, the germ of sadness remains alive. As long as hatred holds one heart, we are all at risk. Fill yourself with drops of joy, and help others find their joy. We're only human. We will occasionally worry, feel bad, or get mad. Indeed, some have said that joy is all the more wonderful because we have felt sorrow.

Sadness is a natural emotion, but once best kept in perspective. Unfortunately, we allow worry to blow many of our frustrations and sorrows out of perspective. In fact, it seems as if some people are so busy worrying, they have forgotten how to be joyful.

Let's help those who are buried by worry, and help

ourselves by crusading for joy. Let us:

> **Laugh** *for the worried; that they may be filled with joy.*
> **Act** *for the worried; that they may know what to do.*
> **Give strength** *to the worried; that they may take heart.*
> **Speak lovingly** *to the worried; for love conquers fear.*
> **Speak lightly** *to the worried; giving them reason to smile.*
> **Speak joyfully** *to the worried; that they find their joy.*

> **Touch the worried with the joy of your spirit**, *and you are as a medicine to their soul. Gladly lend a shoulder to cry on, an ear that will listen, a heart that understands.*
> **Never fear the sorrow of worry;** *one smile is all it takes to scatter a thousand tears.*

> **Sing** *for the worried, smile for the worried, spend time with the worried; give courage to the worried.*
> **Pray** *for the worried. Pray with all the joy that is within you, and you shall be among the blessed.*

Doing this may not seem like taking action, but it is. For when you sing for the worried, when you smile for them, when you give them courage, you make their life a little easier. You're not doing something tangible, you're doing something better. You're changing your attitude toward all the worried people you meet. Instead of responding negatively, you'll understand. You're response will be softer, you'll help guide them toward joy. Help the worried to understand that their cup is filled with joy, and yours will never run dry.

CHAPTER SIX

THE REALITY OF ILLUSION

"The vision of man has the force of a lion."
—English Proverb

One afternoon many years ago a frantic nurse stopped me in a hospital hallway. "Dr. Fox!" she exclaimed. "Mr. Halberstram in 152 is doing push-ups! Make him stop!"

I hurried over to room 152. Mr. Halberstram was indeed on the floor doing push-ups. His back was straight, his head was up as he counted them out: "Thirty-one, thirty-two, thirty-three." Push-ups are great exercise, but Mr. Halberstram had just had a heart attack, he was supposed to be in bed. When I suggested he hop back into bed he replied, without missing a push-up: "Sonny, you're a good doctor, but there are some things you don't know."

I wasn't sure what he was referring to, but since he was obviously going to do his push-ups, I left him alone.

Aside from teenage children, very few people talked back to physicians back then. We were treated with great respect, inside the hospital and out. Older, more traditional nurses even stood up when we entered the room. (This used to bother me. When I asked one nurse, who was old enough to be my mother, to stop standing up every time I came by, she said she would continue to stand as a sign of respect.) Patients were supposed to treat us as demigods, they were supposed to docilely lay in bed, submitting to our prodding, poking, injecting and cutting. In fact, the meekest patients were considered the best patients.

Every once in a great while we'd get a feisty patient, someone who demanded to know exactly what we were doing and why we were doing it, who argued with us and refused to obey our orders. These were considered "bad" patients. The more argumentative they were, the "badder" they were considered to be. I remember one patient named Alex, who gave everyone trouble. Although he was not my patient, I had seen Alex once, a long time ago, when he had had some chest pain. This worried the otherwise healthy, robust man who made a modest living helping to install roofs and insulation. It turned out that the problem was acid splashing up from his stomach, his heart was fine.

Now Alex, a husband and the father of three little girls, was back in the hospital with cancer. Alex was a "bad" patient. When his doctor told him he had a certain number of months to live, Alex insisted that he'd live twice as long. When a nurse tried to interrupt his favorite TV show to give him an injection, Alex politely but firmly ejected her from his room. Hospital food did not suit his palette. He raised such a ruckus, the hospital Administrator finally agreed to have the kitchen cook according to Alex's very detailed specifications. The more the doctors tried to make Alex "behave" himself, the more troublesome he became. When the hospital tried to "solve" the problem by transferring Alex away, he threatened a lawsuit.

Most of the doctors thought that Alex was so difficult because he was a "tough-guy jerk." As a consultant on the case, I saw Alex several times while he was in the hospital. I could see that he was not a mean person. In fact, the way he played with his little girls—which was against the rules, for children were not allowed in patient's rooms back then—suggested that he was a very loving man. He'd have them jumping up and down on his bed, he'd tickle them, he'd throw the littlest one up in the air and she'd squeal with delight. Later on, when the girls had been taken home, there'd be tears in his eyes as he and his wife wondered what would happen to them when he was gone. And there was little doubt that Alex would soon be passing on. Although I believe that we can't "write off" any patient, his cancer was strong, and had spread through his body. Some of the more cynical doctors said that if the cancer didn't get him, the cure, chemotherapy, would. It was just a matter of time, they said.

Curious, I asked Alex why he found hospital rules and traditions tooth-and-nail. "I want to stay in control," he replied.

I thought that was an odd notion. Wasn't he better off surrendering control to the doctors who knew about cancer and surgery and medicines? "Shouldn't you let us handle it?" I asked.

He answered: "Your rules turn patients into rag dolls. I'm not a doctor, so I'll bow to your medical advice. But I want to be in control of my life."

"Why is control so important to you?"

"If I give you doctors control, I'll be dead in six months. That's how much time my cancer doctor says I have left. If I keep control, maybe I can do better."

Alex fought his battle with cancer, his battle for control, to the end. He insisted on hearing full explanations for everything from his doctors, he demanded that his daughters be allowed to visit him, he refused to be interrupted during his favorite TV show, and so on. Even if he was in great pain, he'd refuse to take the prescribed narcotic pain-killers if his daughters were scheduled to visit. It was strange to watch the once-husky man used to earning a living with his hands, now tired and shriveled, playing with his daughters, who were so full of energy and growth.

Finally, Alex was sent home to die. The six month "deadline" his doctor had given him went by and I assumed that

Alex passed away. New patients arrived every day, crises and successes piled one upon another, and the "bad" patient with his three daughters was forgotten.

I don't remember how much time passed—several months, I suppose—when I was asked to consult on another cancer case. I almost laughed out loud when I was handed this new patient's thick chart to study: it was Alex. "This one's a trouble-maker," the new nurse told me. "A real trouble maker."

Alex survived this trip to the hospital, he outlived another "deadline" the doctors solemnly pronounced. Unfortunately, the next trip to the hospital was his last. He didn't leave his daughters much money, if any. I'm sure, however, that he left them the strength that he had to fight for life.

"Healthogenic"

In medical school we studied sick, dying and dead people. We looked at the gross anatomy, the blood, urine, lymph, cerebrospinal fluid. We looked at microscopic slides of tissues taken from people with various diseases. We made pronouncements and came to conclusions based on our observations. When I first came to the Los Angeles County Hospital in 1958, I spent long, almost surrealistic nights in wards filled with people who had swollen bodies, very thin arms and legs, yellow skin, who were confused, thrashing around, tied into beds, vomiting up blood onto my clean white uniform and dying of hepatic (liver) coma. I thought that every one in Los Angeles was an alcoholic, was destined to develop cirrhosis and then liver failure, and much worse, keep me up for 36-48 hours at a time trying vainly to save them.

This was and is the way doctors learned, the *pathogenic* (disease-causing) method. Look at the sickies. How did they live, how did they become ill, how did they die? Disease was exciting, and was simple to see. Find the myocardial infarction (heart attack), the coronary thrombosis (blood clot in a coronary artery), the chronic bronchitis (often the end result of cigarette smoking or occupational exposure to chemicals or particles), the thyroid cancer (often from exposure to radioactive iodine or other substances), the mesothelioma (a cancer due to asbestos exposure many years before), the stress-induced high blood pressure, the tuberculosis (from exposure to the germ mycobacteria tuberculosis). Identify and classify the pathology. But what about the people who are exposed to the same germs, chemicals, stress, etcetera, yet remain healthy? What about the healthy people?

I began gradually to look for another way to view my patients, and people in general. I arrived at the *healthogenic* (health-causing) view, the idea that studying healthy people is just as illuminating as studying the disease. Perhaps more so. For example, why is it that about one-third of Nazi Concentration Camp survivors who suffered years of malnutrition, forced labor, horribly unsanitary conditions, physical abuse and the constant threat of death were healthy years later, while so many of the other survivors were ill? What is it about those one-third?

Many Vietnam vets went through the horrors of battle, seeing their friends blown apart, but only some suffering lasting emotional trauma. Why? I've had patients into whom we poured 20-30 pints of blood while they bled out the same amount in a short time. They had multiple problems including kidney failure, congestive heart failure, shock, severe anxiety and depression. They were physically, emotionally and mentally stressed, yet they recovered to live a full life. Others, often with lesser diseases, succumbed and became pathologic specimens in the autopsy lab.

Oh yes, there were the risk-factors I could look at, such as high cholesterol, obesity, elevated blood pressure, cigarettes, alcohol, diabetes, and so on. These standard risk factors were not always very illuminating. After all, back then a lot of middle-aged men smoked cigarettes, drank too much alcohol, were overweight, didn't exercise and had high blood pressure. Some had diabetes mellitus and a family history of heart attack. Others did not. Some had a very high cholesterol, some were mildly high, while others had normal levels. The standard risk factors did not explain anything.

What was I missing? I was signing five, six, even seven death certificates a week. I used to wonder if anyone in the state capitol was keeping score. I wondered if they'd say, "Wow! That Dr. Fox is our #1 man." Actually, many of the certificates I signed were for people who were DOA (dead on arrival), or almost DOA. Clearly, the pathogenic approach left much to be desired. In the 1970s I fought a seemingly one-man battle with my colleagues to get stress (that is, dis-stress) included as an important risk factor for coronary artery disease and other illnesses. I crusaded to get people to change their diet, exercise and reduce the stress in their lives. That helped, but there was still something missing. High cholesterol, elevated blood pressure, cigarettes, alcohol and other factors were pathogenic. Healthful eating, exercise and stress reduction were healthogenic. Still, something was missing.

Now, bolstered by many new studies, I am convinced that in many cases, "illusion" was the missing something. Illusion, something that is not so, can be a tremendous medicine. Having said that illusion is important, let me back up for a moment and speak about the medicine called "control." Then we'll come back to "illusion."

Turn It Down!

Lying in a hospital bed, fighting what seemed a losing battle against cancer, Alex wanted to be in control of as much of his life as he could. Even if it was just a question of what brand of jello he ate, he wanted to be in control. Many interesting studies have examined this idea of control. Although some researchers have come to different conclusions, I believe that control is as important to our health as is good food. For example, if you give laboratory animals electric shocks, you will damage their immune systems.[1] But if you give the rats some control over the shocks, for example, let them press a lever to avoid some of the shock, their immune systems won't suffer as much. The animals still receive shocks, but they have some control. Just having even a little control bolsters their health.

In a fascinating study,[2] researchers at the University of Wisconsin divided monkeys into three groups. The first group was forced to listen to terribly noxious noise, but given some control. A retractable lever was presented at certain specified times. By pushing the lever, the monkeys could turn the awful noise off.

The second group listened to the same noise, for the same amount of time, but was not allowed to turn it off.

The third group, the control group, did not have to listen to the noise.

High-intensity noise is stressful, especially the kind these poor monkeys were forced to endure: The sounds of power tools running, heavy machinery, drills, snowmobiles, and so on. Thirteen minutes of noise, two minutes of silence: The monkeys listened to four full cycles, lasting an hour overall.

---

1 Electric shock can cause their lymphocyte proliferation rate to drop. Lymphocytes are important members of the immune system "army." Their ability to increase (proliferate) in response to a challenge is a measure of immune system strength.
2 Janson, JD et al.: The Effects of Control over High Intensity Noise on Plasma Cortisol Levels in Rhesus Monkeys. Behav. Bio. 16, 333-340 (1976), Abstract No. 5217.

As you would expect, the awful racket upset the animals. Elevated cortisol levels, a sign of stress, were found in the blood of monkeys who had no control over the noise, who had no choice but to listen and hope it would end soon. Not only that, the monkeys who had no control interacted with each other much less after being exposed to the noise. Physically (elevated cortisol) and behaviorally (less social contact), noise harmed the monkeys who had no control.

But for the monkeys with control over the noise, the ones who pushed the lever to shut it off, cortisol (stress) levels *did not* rise significantly, and social behavior *was not disturbed* (compared to quiet times). Having control—even only some— was as effective as a medicine.

Perception is Reality

Having control is important. So is *feeling* that you're in control. Many great thinkers have said words to the effect of "If you think you can, you're right. If you think you can't, you're also right." They know that our belief influences our performance. Those who believe they're in control of the situation, or can gain control, generally do a lot better than those who are convinced that the events are beyond their control. Positive thinking leads to positive action.

Among my childhood playmates, the ones who succeeded were mostly the ones who believed they would. It wasn't the smartest of my college and medical school buddies who got the best grades, it was those who believed they could. Physical talent is important, but among all the Little Leaguers my sons and I have coached, the ones who believed they were Babe Ruth generally became the best hitters.

Researchers have looked at children, control and belief. Even when they're failing, children who believe that they are in control of the situation, and believe in themselves, perform better than children who consider themselves failures. In one interesting study,[3] children were divided into two groups based on personality traits, the "positive" group and "negative" group. All the children were then asked to answer questions based on shapes drawn on cards. The test was rigged so that after some initial success, the children began to fail.

In the early part of the test, the part in which all the children were allowed to succeed, both the "positive" and the "negative" children did well. This suggests that both groups, "positive" and "negative," were equally smart. When they got to the rigged part of the test, however, and began to fail, the differences in their attitudes and performances were striking.

When the going got tough, the "positive" children thought they were failing because they weren't trying hard enough. All they had to do, they believed and said, was try harder, concentrate more, and they'll get it right. They'd say "I love a challenge," and "I've almost got it now." They'd try new strategies, new approaches to the problem. A fair number of the "positive" children continued to predict success for themselves, even though they were failing. They felt they were in control of the situation, or could gain control with some effort.

The "negative" children, on the other hand, often gave up. They would say that they couldn't possibly succeed because they had bad memories, they'd say that they were confused. They tended to stick with the same strategies that weren't working, and their performance took a nose-dive. They dwelled on their failure. They wanted to walk away from the problem. The "positive" children, on the other hand, focused on the success they already had, and on the successes they felt they were soon going to enjoy. They emphasized the positive. They tried harder. They tried new ways.

---

3 Diener, CI and Dweck, CS.: An Analysis of Learned Helplessness: Continuous Changes in Performance, Strategy, and Achievement Cognitions Following Failure. J. Personality and Social Psy. 1978, 36, 451-462.

The kids were equally talented. Perception was the difference. The ones that felt they were in control, or could be in control, outperformed the others. I saw something very similar happen many years ago, when Barry, my son and co-author, was young. Barry was not a very good baseball batter. I remember watching Barry's first "Pee-Wee League" game at Sunnyslope Park in Monterey Hills. He struck out four times, dropped the only ball hit to him in the outfield, and cried. Fortunately, the season was short. Unfortunately, he kept striking out while playing with the boys on the block, some of whom laughed at him. But Barry was a "positive" boy. He believed that although he was doing very poorly, he was in control. All through the winter he practiced, hitting little stones with a stick in our backyard. When spring rolled around and the neighborhood kids picked teams for their first game, Barry was chosen last.

That was the last time he was chosen last, because, as it turned out, no one could strike him out. He hit everything the pitchers threw at him, and he hit it "where they ain't," carefully placing the ball in between, over, around and through the fielders. He finished the Little League season as his team's Most Valuable Player and a member of the All-Star Team. It was a winter's worth of practice that made the difference, but he only practiced because he believed he was in control, or could be in control, of his life.

A thirty-five year study of Harvard College graduates from the 1940s looked at this same issue. The students were grouped according to how they explained the bad things that happened to them in their business and personal lives, as members of the Armed Forces having to fight a war, and so on. Some blamed their problems—and we all have our problems— by referring to their own negative qualities: *they blamed themselves*. The ones who blamed themselves for their difficulties were less healthy years later than the ones who did not blame themselves. Pessimistic young adults had a greater risk of becoming sick oldsters than the optimistic young adults did.[4]

Who's Really in Control—and Does It Matter?

The idea that being in control of your life can help make you healthier and more successful makes sense. But are we really in control as often as we think we are? And does it matter?

The "positive" kids who outperformed their "negative" friends were not really in control: The test was rigged so everyone would succeed in the beginning, and fail later on. The researchers were running the show, not the children.

What about those monkeys, the ones who stopped the noise by pressing the lever? It turns out that they really didn't have much control at all. They only thought they did. You see, the retractable lever, the one they pushed to turn the noise off, was not slid into the little room until the noise was just about scheduled to end anyway. (There were four cycles of thirteen minutes of noise, each followed by two minutes of silence. The lever was not presented until the thirteen minutes were just about up.) The monkeys were well-trained, they pushed the lever as soon as they saw it. *But the noise was going to end soon whether or not they actually pushed it.* They only had the illusion of control. Believing they were in control made a physical and emotional difference, for the better.

An Added Note on Control

The monkey/noise researchers delved deeper by taking control away from the monkeys who had been taught to push

---

4 Peterson, C. et al.: Pessimistic Explanatory Style is a Risk Factor for Physical Illness: A 35 Year Longitudinal Study. Journal of Personality & Social Psychology, 55: 23-27, 1988.

the lever. The monkeys listened to the same noise, for the same amount of time. The lever was slid into the cage at intermittent times, but when the monkeys pressed it, nothing happened. The loss-of-control group suffered heavily. Compared to quiet times, their cortisol (stress) levels during noisy periods jumped up. Some became quite aggressive, as well.

Not being bothered at all is ideal, whether we're monkeys or humans. But if we have to be bothered, it's best to have some kind of control over the problem, even if the control is mostly in our heads. Worst of all is losing the control we once had.

The Reality of Illusion

Early on in this chapter I said that illusion can be a powerful medicine. The monkeys had the illusion of control. So did the "positive" kids. The monkeys were given the illusion by the scientists. The kids made up the illusion on their own. They apparently went through life deceiving themselves, pretending. Their pretense was positive. It helped them to succeed, so in a sense, it wasn't a deception at all. It was real.

We say that those who believe in illusions are crazy. After all, we should all be absolutely rational and realistic, right? Which group was more realistic, the "positive" kids or the "negative" kids? They were taking the same test, at the same time, in the same place. The difference was perception. Illusion is perception. Now, when I speak of illusions, I don't mean seeing pink elephants dancing on your dashboard, believing that you are Napoleon, or jumping off a building because you think you can fly. No, I'm talking about the kind of illusion that comes from your positive perception, the type of illusion that prompts you into positive action.

When the doctors told my grandfather that he had X number of months left to live, his answer was defiant: "The doctors, what do they know?" He continued working until the end of his life, which was a lot longer than the doctor predicted. He had an illusion. The cold, hard, precise "facts" of medical science said he was slated to die soon. Imminent death was the "reality." He saw things differently. His illusion became his reality. He said he would outlive his doctors, and he did.

Mr. Halberstram, the patient who scandalized the hospital by doing push-ups shortly after his heart attack, was defying "reality." Reality said he should be in bed. But he had an illusion, an illusion of health. His illusion became his reality.

A patient once came to my office, excitedly requesting those "magic weight-loss shots" he heard about. I told him I didn't have any magic weight-loss shot, but he insisted that I did. He said that I had given the shots to a friend of his, and that the guy had lost fifty pounds. We went back and forth for a while before I agreed to give him the "magic weight-loss shots." I gave him instruction for dieting and told him to come to the office once a week for several weeks. Then I told my nurse to give him a saline (salt water) injection every time he came in. She was also to weigh him and, no matter what he weighed, tell him that the doctor was very disappointed with him. It was all an illusion, there was no "magic weight-loss shot." But you know what? He lost a lot of weight, fast, and kept it off. His illusion became his reality.

Illusion is perception. Grandfather thought he was going to be healthy. The "positive" children believed they were going to succeed. Because so much of what happens to us in life is subject to our perception, illusion can become our reality.

What illusions should we have? There are many. Even in the face of evidence to the contrary, you should believe that:

- *You can do it.*
- *You're in control of your life.*
- *Your life is meaningful.*
- *Your life is manageable.*
- *Life is great.*
- *People are basically good.*
- *If things are bad now, they'll get better.*
- *You **can** make a difference.*

Are these illusions? Perhaps they are, at the moment, for you. But remember: *Illusions have a way of becoming reality.*

SOC

I guess it seems as if we've wandered around in this chapter, touching upon one patient doing push-ups, another who wanted to control his life, monkeys pushing levers and children taking a test, illusions and reality. What is the connection?

The idea we're trying to get across in our roundabout fashion is this: *Believing that you're in control of your life is a powerful medicine—even if you're not in control. The feeling of control can help make you healthier, happier, and more successful in every way.*

My Grandfather always felt that he was in control of his life. Was he? Objectively speaking, not really, not much. Perched low on the economic ladder, he was liable to be kicked down a few rungs at any time. Life-long hard work was absolutely necessary. He had no influence on government or politics. True, he was well-known and respected in our community, but ours was a small circle. Still, Grandfather felt himself to be the master of his fate. How could that be?

Things made sense to Grandfather. He knew who he was.

He understood life, as he interpreted it. He felt that he had a role, small but important, to play. He believed that he could perform his assigned duties, and that he would be rewarded for doing so after he had passed on. These qualities were assembled, distilled and described in a somewhat different, yet compelling way by A. Antonovsky in his recent book, *Unraveling the Mystery of Health*.[5] Antonovsky argued that people with a strong *"Sense of Coherence"* (*SOC*) are more likely than others to be emotionally and physically healthy:

> *"This sense of coherence is a global orientation that expresses the extent to which one has a pervasive, enduring though dynamic feeling of confidence that:*
>
> 1. *the struggle deriving from one's internal and external environments in the course of living are structured, predictable and explainable;*
> 2. *the resources are available for one to meet the demands posed by these stimuli;*
> 3. *these demands are looked upon as challenges worthy of investment and engagement."*[6]

In other words, if you believe that life is *understandable, manageable*, and *meaningful*, you have a Sense of Coherence. Life makes sense to you. You believe you can do what is necessary, you can play your role, you can overcome most, if not all, obstacles. Finally, you feel that there is some purpose to your life, that in the end, you've made a difference. And may I add, the Sense of Coherence comes strictly from your perception, and your feeling. No one can say that "objectively" speaking, you do or do not have a Sense of Coherence. That's entirely up to you.

5 Antonovsky, A. *Unraveling The Mystery of Health*. San Francisco: Jossey-Bass, 1987.
6 Antonovsky, A: The "Sense of Cohesion" Concept, in Unraveling the Mystery of Health: How People Manage Stress and Stay Well (by A. Antonovsky) Jossey-Bass, San Francisco, 1987 (p. 191)

Grandfather had a great Sense of Coherence. Alex, the "bad" patient, was groping toward his Sense of Coherence. The "positive" children taking the rigged test had a Sense of Coherence, which the "negative" kids lacked.

An understandable, manageable and meaningful life: That's the SOC recipe.

1. Understandable: Explainable, comprehensible. My grandfather and others like him had suffered through war, famine, death, financial disasters and more, but felt there was a reason for everything. In Grandfather's mind, everything that happened was an opportunity given to him by God to learn something, to grow, or to experience the bitter as well as the sweet aspects of life. He especially looked upon the loss of a loved one as God's way of reminding us that love, family and friends are more dear to us than houses, jewelry and money.

2. Manageable: That comes from the feeling that you have, or can develop, the skills or power to handle most of what comes along. You believe that you are reliable and capable. You are oriented toward a goal or goals. You are able to work independently, and feel that you can handle the pressure. You optimistically organize and work to solve problems, not ruminate endlessly about them. You're confident that you can always stay afloat, even if the seas be stormy. I know that Grandfather always believed that because God was his ally, he couldn't possibly lose.

When you believe that life is manageable, you know that we're all going to win a few, and lose a few. You realize that bad things do sometimes happen to good people, but you don't dwell on the negatives. You know that the answers come much more readily to those who focus on the positive, on the possibilities. Must you have all the resources to manage life lined up before you can feel that life is manageable? No, the perception alone is enough. You'll pick up the skills and tools necessary to manage life as you move along. But you may never get started if you wait until everything is guaranteed before making your first move.

3. Meaningful: What does life and what do events mean to you? Is it all drudgery, or is there a sense of accomplishment in your work and/or hobbies, a feeling of joy from spending time with your children, a moment of sympathy when you lend someone your shoulder to cry on? Feeling that life is worth living, that life is filled with opportunity to give and share joy, builds a Sense of Coherence.

Having an understandable, manageable and meaningful life = a Sense of Coherence = Better emotional and physical health, plus a head start on success. And you know what? It can all be an illusion. Nobody can tell us if our life is understandable, manageable and meaningful. It's all a matter of perception. It's all a matter of how we see things. We control our perception, so we're in control. We determine whether or not we have a Sense of Coherence. *Feel* that life is worthwhile, and it will become so.

Life is understandable, manageable and meaningful to me. When I was a poor student, wondering where I could get the money to pay rent and to feed my family, life was understandable, manageable and meaningful. When, later in life, bad business decisions and a devastating fire practically wiped me out, life was still understandable, manageable and meaningful. Was it an illusion? "Realistically" speaking, I should have felt that life was incomprehensible, unmanageable and absolutely meaningless: My children were helping my wife and I pay our rent, my underinsured-practice went up in flames set by an arsonist, and I was fighting yet another up-hill battle to get my medical colleagues to recognize the importance of stress. Was my Sense of Coherence an illusion? Absolutely not! I believed it, therefore, it was so. My interpretation was the only "reality" that counted.

It doesn't even matter if we can "prove" that someone doesn't have the resources to make life manageable. Remember the "positive" children taking the test. The test was rigged so that they *had* to fail. Objectively speaking, life was not manageable for them at that moment. But they felt it was, and their illusion was the only "reality" that counted.

Gail's Doll House

Making sense out of life can be difficult. Think how tough it might be for someone who wasn't born with all the blessings we take for granted. I've known a handicapped woman named Gail for a little while. Although she is mentally handicapped by a mind that does not work as well as it should, she has a strong Sense of Coherence. Gail delights in her successes, and she keeps her failures in perspective. That's not as easy as it sounds, for her successes are few and far between, while her failures are many. But if we were to read the book of her memory, I'm sure we would find her successes written in bold letters, circled in red, with the failures written in tiny letters, off in the margins.

Gail tackles each new task with energy and enthusiasm, though she knows the going will be slow. Nothing comes easy to her, nothing but her beautiful smile. Her parents, their minds filled with the great dreams all parents have for their children, had a difficult time accepting the fact that their first-born child was "slow." Although they were good people, they found it easier to concentrate on their other children, who were all bright, and let the "special school" handle Gail. But Gail was not content to remain on the sidelines all her life, condescended to, treated like a child. She told me that for years she was very sad, that she felt "like left-overs." She wanted to own her own doll shop, but knew that was but an idle dream. Then one day, she said, she suddenly knew why she had been born with a handicap, and she knew what she must do: "My job is to prove that everyone can make it by making it myself. It's to inspire others to go for it."

The teachers at her school were very nice, but they "knew" that she was "slow," and shouldn't hope for much. They were very interested in teaching Gail and her classmates basic skills. When Gail said she wanted to own her own shop, she wanted to learn about shopkeeping, they smiled and said "Yes, yes, that's very nice dear," and tried to steer her toward clerical work. They never told her "no, you can't be a shopkeeper." But they never said "yes," either. In many subtle ways, they constantly discouraged her.

But Gail refused to be held back. She knew what her job was, and she was determined to do it. When she was fifteen she went out, on her own, and got a part-time job dusting the shelves, moving merchandise and running errands for a little neighborhood knick-knack shop. She kept asking the owner questions: How do you know what to order? How do you set prices? How do you make up a display? How do you do the bookkeeping? A kindly old man, the owner answered all her questions, patiently going over and over the procedures. When he passed away and the shop closed up, Gail endured countless turndowns before finding another low-level job in a store. That job didn't work out, so she moved on to another, always determined to learn all there was to know about being a shopkeeper. She found herself another job in a small clothing store with a sympathetic owner. Her new boss, a woman named Mona, patiently taught Gail all about the merchandise, ordering, displays, pricing, bookkeeping, and so on. Mona didn't know anything about teaching the handicapped, like Gail's teachers did. All she knew about teaching was to always be kind.

One day, when Gail came to work, Mona pinned a little badge on her blouse. It said: "Assistant Manager."

"I was so proud I cried," Gail said. "But that's when I knew I was going to have my own doll shop."

How was Gail going to get her own shop? She had saved all her money, but it wasn't nearly enough. Her parents didn't have the money to buy her a shop. Gail said that there was never any doubt in her mind that she would have a shop. "Getting the money was just another problem to beat," she explained. "I had learned what I had to do to beat the other problems, so I could beat this one, too."

She enrolled in a bookkeeping and a marketing class at the local junior college. She had to read the text books three times apiece, she had to tape the lectures and listen to them again and again, but that didn't stop her. Gail told everyone she knew about her dream: Friends, family, customers, suppliers, her teachers and classmates, everybody.

A long time passed with no progress toward her shop. Then one of the customers at the shop where she worked told Gail that she would give her $500 toward Gail's doll shop, *if* somebody else would also invest in Gail. Excited beyond belief, Gail found another investor. Then Mona, her boss, offered her a little shelf space in the clothing store. With the investment money, Gail's own savings, and three rows of dolls on borrowed shelf space, "Gail's Doll House" was born.

Gail said that the day she opened "Gail's Doll House," everything seemed to make sense to her. Her life was understandable, manageable and meaningful. She knew that her job was to inspire others to succeed by showing them her example, and she knew that one way or another, she could do it.

"Gail's Doll House" eventually outgrew it's first home. It found a new home in a little shop, tended by Gail the shopkeeper. "I'm not a left-over anymore," she says. "I'm a shopkeeper. I did it. Anybody can do it."

I don't know if just anyone can do it. It may take someone
with Gail's special talents.

R_x: POSITIVE PERCEPTION

Gail once told me that she keeps a shoebox full of small,
brightly-colored polished stones in a drawer in her apartment.
Every morning she sets the box on a table, opens it up, and
thrusts both her hands into the box, grabbing two big handfuls
of brightly-colored stones. She holds those stones tightly,
gazing at what she calls her handfuls of potential.

"Each stone is something I can do," she told me. "Each
stone is also something I've done right, and it's something else
I'm going to do right, soon."

It's an amazing idea; she actually holds onto her potential,
seeing it simultaneously as the good things she's done, and the
great things she's going to do. Then, to symbolize her control
over her life, she then lays several of the little stones on the
table, one at a time, forming a circle. Putting each stone into
place emphasizes that she determines the patterns of her life.
She chose the circle as her pattern, she explained, because a
circle has no beginning and no end. She believes that her
success, like the circle, will continue forever.

Can "failures" or "negative" thinkers who are convinced
they'll never succeed learn to think success? Can they take
control of their lives? Yes. I've seen it happen many times. If
Gail can do it, we can, too. And remember, that's Gail's "job"
in life—to show us that we can do it.

Let's symbolize our control the way Gail does. Go out and
buy a bunch of small, polished stones. You can get them in
hobby shops and other stores. Or go outside and pick up a
couple handfuls of smooth stones, or use checkers, match-

sticks or something similar.

Begin your day by grabbing up two handfuls of stones. Look up to them: These are yesterday's successes, these are tomorrow's potential. Now slowly lay the stones into a small circle on a table or countertop, one stone at a time as you say:

Life is composed of many steps
Some large, some small.
Each step takes me to the next.
I may not know how many twists and turns lie ahead,
But I know that there always is a way.

Making Illusions Real

Susan's father deserted her and her mother when Susan was just a few years old. When Susan was five her mother suffered a nervous breakdown and, unable to care for her daughter, turned her over to the authorities. So began Susan's long odyssey, from one foster home to another. Living in some fifteen homes in twelve years left Susan feeling like a piece of drift wood tossed about by the ocean waves, never knowing where she was headed next, never feeling solid ground under her feet, not knowing whether she was above water or below. Just before her seventeenth birthday Susan was sent to a new foster home. This would probably be her last, for once she was eighteen she was on her own. When the social worker brought Susan to her new home, she took the new parents aside and said: "Don't expect too much from her."

Although a pleasant girl, Susan was a poor student, and like many teenagers of the time, she tried this drug and that. As the social worker said, "Don't expect too much from her."

Over dinner, Susan's new parents asked what she would like to be. Susan replied: "I'd like to be a doctor, but I'm not smart enough."

"What do you mean, not smart enough?" her new father asked.

"Not smart enough. I only get 'C's' in science, I almost flunked calculus. I'm not smart enough. Ask my social worker, she'll tell you I'm not very smart."

"I think you're smart enough," said the new mother. "Life has pushed you around. Now it's time to take the bull by the horns and tell life what's what."

"But there's too much to do," Susan protested.

"Break it into little steps," her mother advised. "Bring your grades up by studying every night and on Saturday, and going to summer school. Prepare for college entrance tests by taking one of the study courses. Research colleges, figure out which one you want to go to. Then set up two alternate colleges, in case you don't get into your first choice. Let's find a doctor who will let you go to his office and learn a little. And most important of all, set your goals. Figure out which medical school you want to go to. For the next five years, everything you do will be aimed at getting you there."

That seems like a tall order for a girl who used to be kicked out of her home at a moment's notice, but Susan took control. She divided her life into manageable tasks and she set her goal. She knew that everything positive she did carried her closer to her goal.

Five years is a long time for a young person such as Susan. Coming after many years of frustration, five years of schooling can be difficult, especially when you have no family to back you up. Fortunately, Susan's last set of foster parents stuck with her, gave her a place to call home, somewhere to go during vacations, a little extra money now and then. And they kept reminding her to "take the bull by the horns." Set your goals, they told her. Divide the impossible into smaller, more manageable tasks. Most of all, believe in yourself.

Today Susan is a medical doctor, a heart surgeon, a professor, and a chief of staff at a major hospital. The "Don't expect too much from her" girl remade her reality by taking control.

Set your goals. Chop your impossibles into manageable parts. Turn your dreams into reality by taking control.

CHAPTER SEVEN

STICKITIVITUITY

"Big shots are only little shots who keep shooting."
—Christopher Morley

Back in the 1970s I occasionally jogged with a fiftyish man named Lewis around the track on the seventh floor of the Los Angeles Athletic Club. Tall and handsome, a natural athlete, the son of a college professor and a former model, Lewis referred to himself as the "worst failure that ever lived."

"I'd call myself the best failure that ever lived," he said, "but that would imply that I'm good at something, even if the something is failing. So I call myself the worst failure."

If you pursued the subject Lewis would tell you that he was a pretty quick failure. "I used to try a lot before I realized I wasn't going to get anywhere," he said. "Now I give up right away, because I know what's going to happen."

Lewis had dropped out of college because his grades were too low to get him into a good law school. He flirted with the idea of being a stand-up comic, but gave that up after being booed off the stage several times. His parents bought him a small business which he closed up after making some bad business decisions, having problems with his suppliers and with the Internal Revenue Service. He wrote two novels, but twenty-some rejections from publishers convinced him to forget about being an author.

"The only thing I'm good at is sensing failure," Lewis used to brag. "I've got a sixth sense for impending doom. That's good, because I don't waste energy trying too long on things that are going to fail, which is most things for me."

Lewis was a witty man. You had to laugh at the way he recounted the stories of his failure. But while you were laughing outside you cried a little inside, for you knew that Lewis was hurting, despite his smile. You could hear it in his voice, you could see it in his face when, every so often, he let his smile drop.

Lewis stopped coming to the club, I didn't see him for a couple months. Then one day when I went to the hospital to examine a patient, I saw Lewis. He was lying in the bed next to my patient. Lewis told me that he had cancer, and that he was going to die. "I've tried chemotherapy," he said mournfully, "but I failed. That's typical for me." He smiled a weak smile as he added: "I'm still the worst failure around."

I don't know if chemotherapy would have cured Lewis, or perhaps kept him alive for several years. The odds were good, considering his type of cancer, his otherwise good health, his strong physical condition and age. But Lewis "knew" there was no point trying. He "knew" he was going to fail in his fight against cancer. His negative attitude made his cancer stronger, and the medicine weaker. I don't know the details of the case, for Lewis was not my patient. I do know that he wasn't in the hospital very long, and it wasn't long before I heard from the others at the club that Lewis had passed away. I guess, in a strange sense, the worst failure had finally done something well.

DOWN BUT NOT OUT

"The man who wins may have been counted
out several times, but he didn't hear the referee"
—H.E. Jansen

As a young boy growing up in South Philadelphia, I knew every little nook and cranny in my neighborhood. I knew who lived in which house, what they did and where they came from. I knew which alley to go through and which fence to hop over to get somewhere quicker. I also knew, because it was very important to know, the ethnic boundaries.

At that time, the different immigrant groups huddled together for protection; they lived, worked, worshipped and played together in their crowded "ghettos." The Irish had the area from the Delaware River to 3rd Street. To the south were the real tough, and very poor, Scots-Irish. To the west were the Italians. There was a Jewish neighborhood; there were pockets of Polish immigrants, Czechoslovakian immigrants, and so on. You knew when you crossed the boundaries, you could tell by the sights, the sounds, the smells. And, if you were a boy or young man, you knew that when you crossed the line you were in "enemy territory." If the "locals" saw you, fists might fly.

One day when I was eight or nine years old, three ethnic boys beat me up when I wandered into their neighborhood. Scared and hurt, I ran home crying, the three boys chasing me all the way. They would have followed me into my home and continued beating me if my father had not stepped out just as I dashed up the steps. The boys skidded to a halt as I tried to dive between my father's legs. But he stopped me. He stood me up, turned me around, then none-too-gently threw me down the steps with an order: "Don't come back until you beat them up."

I was more frightened of my father than of the boys so, crying, I went down the steps. Determined to win because I didn't want to have to face my father, I threw my fists out. By accident I hit the biggest of the boys in the nose. He started crying and ran away. I started hitting the other two and before I knew it, I was chasing *them* back to their neighborhood.

What had changed? The three of them were still stronger

than me. But now I refused to give up. Some years later I found myself in yet another losing battle, this time with a real tough guy who kept knocking me down. (Luckily, back then we had a code—no guns, no knives, no hitting anyone when they're down, and so on.) He kept knocking me down, bloodied my nose, and bruised every part of me there was to bruise, but I kept getting up. He'd knock me down, I'd get up. Finally he asked: "What will it take to make you surrender?"

"You'll have to kill me," I replied.

You know what? He walked away. He saw that although he was a much better fighter than I was, I was not going to give up. I didn't win that fight. But because I refused to give up, I didn't lose it, either. (Please don't get the impression that I'm in favor of fighting. I'm not. I don't even know what we were fighting about most of the time, and I later became friends with most of the boys I fought with.)

Lewis, the "worst failure that ever lived," was a talented, educated man. He could have been successful in many ways, but he lacked "stickiness." He didn't' stick with anything long enough to succeed. He didn't get topnotch grades in college. Plenty of great men and women had difficulties in school. Thomas Edison and Albert Einstein were considered poor students. He couldn't get into the best law school. There are plenty of other good schools. Besides, relatively few attorneys go to the best schools. Most go to mid-level law schools.

Booed off the stage? The list of performers booed off the stage in their early years goes on forever. Two of my favorites, George Burns and the Marx Brothers, struggled for years before "making it."

Bad business decisions? Two very famous business embarrassments were committed by huge companies backed by armies of experts: Ford lost a bundle on its Edsel, and Coca-Cola goofed with its "new" Coke. The history of bad business decisions made by companies large and small would fill volumes.

Business problems with his suppliers and the Internal Revenue Service? That's par for the course. (Barry once spent three years on my behalf trying to convince the I.R.S. that I was only one person, not two, and should only pay tax for one person.)

Rejection letters from publishers? Most every author I know, including Barry and I, has files stuffed full of rejection letters. Rudyard Kipling, considered one of the greats, author of *The Jungle Book*, received a rejection letter that said, among other things, "you just don't know how to use the English language." Best-selling author Frederick Forsyth was told by a publisher that his book "had no reader interest." The book was *The Day of the Jackal,* which sold over eight million copies. A publisher informed Richard Bach that his *Jonathan Livingston Seagull* would never sell as a paperback. I wonder if that publisher knows that *Jonathan Livingston Seagull* sold over seven million copies in paperback? Daniel Defoe's *Robinson Crusoe* was turned down by numerous publishers.

And Lewis' cancer? Well, one can never say for sure, but I'm convinced that Lewis died so quickly because he believed he would. He knew that he couldn't fight back. He knew that he was a failure, the fastest failure around.

I'm not writing this because I know so much, or because I never give in. I do surrender sometimes. We all do. It's part of being human. And I believe that sometimes it's smarter to back down, at least for the moment. The point, as Henry David Thoreau and General George Patton and so many others have said, is that success is often just a matter of hanging on a little bit longer.

REAL ESTATE, REAL DETERMINATION

> *"The only good luck many great men*
> *ever had was being born with the ability and*
> *determination to overcome bad luck."*
>   —Channing Pollock

One of my patients was a twenty-eight year old woman named Lucy, a wife and mother of two little girls. Lucy and her husband Tom, like many lower-middle class families, were deeply in debt. They lived from paycheck to paycheck, always struggling to pay the rent, never able to put away much money for emergencies. Their credit cards were stretched to the limit, they had borrowed from their parents (who didn't have much to spare). But they had hope. Lucy wanted to be a real estate "wheeler-dealer." She planned to begin by buying a run-down little house, which she and Tom would fix-up, then sell for a profit. Then they'd buy a house to rent out, find some undeveloped land to buy and sell, and move up to owning small apartment buildings, eventually owning properties all over the city. In fact, Lucy had just passed the state test and begun working as a real estate salesperson. She and Tom spoke excitedly for hours about how she would find their first fixer-upper and they'd be on their way.

Their lives seemed to fall apart when Tom, a construction worker, fell off the roof of a house he was working on. His meager disability payments weren't enough to keep them going. Like many injured workers, Tom was abandoned by his former employer. He might have been eligible for more money, but first the attorneys had to argue over whether he had suffered this or that percentage disability.

Lucy had begun selling real estate part-time shortly before Tom was injured at work, but the economy was down and the market was terrible. Few houses were selling, and those that did sell were sold by the experienced salespeople with contacts, not newcomers like Lucy. Lucy needed money right now to keep the roof over her family's head. She had to sell some houses. But where were the buyers?

Lucy left flyers on all the doorknobs in the neighborhood. She spoke at the community clubs, telephoned home owners, did everything one was supposed to do in order to find clients. She studied the neighborhoods and went to all the open houses in order to learn everything there was to learn about the houses in her city. She drove the few clients she did have all around the city, trying to sell them a house. The two sales she arranged fell apart because the buyers couldn't get home loans. Home owners were desperate to sell, and she wanted to make a deal, but buyers with money were scarce.

Everyday brought new unhappy news to Lucy and Tom. The landlord was threatening to evict them because they weren't paying their rent. Their credit cards were cancelled. Collections agencies called day and night. Their parents had no more money to give to them. Tom's car was repossessed. His injury was not improving, and he had constant headaches. Desperate to keep a roof over her family's head, Lucy worked nights at a liquor store. All day long she pounded the pavements looking for buyers to match with sellers. Six hours a night, five nights a week she warily eyed every customer who came into the liquor store, wondering if they were going to pull a wallet or a gun out of their pockets.

Tom tried to make cabinets to sell in the garage, but was in too much pain to work for more than a few hours a day. Luckily their two daughters were too young to know they were liable to lose their house. They wondered why they didn't see much of mommy anymore, but were glad to have daddy home, even if he did lay on the couch a lot.

The bad news mounted as Lucy pounded the pavements. They had to apply for food stamps and other aid. The manager at the real estate office threatened to fire Lucy if she didn't produce. Everyone was telling Lucy to give it up, file for bankruptcy protection and get a job as a waitress.

"I didn't want to give up," Lucy said, "because I knew that if I stuck to it, sooner or later I would make the first sale. And the first would lead to the second and the third, if I could just stick to it. The point is to stick to it.

"When things were really bad, when I'd just sit in my car and cry, I'd think about how good I was going to feel when I got that first commission check. Thinking about it kept me going. I knew I had to stick to it."

Not only did she stick to it, Lucy also took on the "Nobuys." No-buys, she explained, are the people who say they want to buy a house, but are never satisfied with anything you show them. Everything you show them is too big or too small, too old or too new, too close to a main street or too far from the main street. Every house is too expensive, or needs too much work, has too many rooms or not enough rooms. It has the wrong kind of roof. It gets too much morning sun, or not enough. It doesn't have enough room in the back yard for the dog, or the neighborhood isn't right. If it has a gas stove, the No-buys want electricity. It's too close to a school, or too far from the market.

Naturally enough, the salespeople in Lucy's office quickly abandoned the No-buys. Lucy kept her No-buys, and added all the other No-buys to her list of clients. Her coworkers told her she was wasting her time, but Lucy felt that if she stuck to it, she could even sell a No-buy a house. But how could she stick to it, she wondered, when they were about to be tossed out on to the street?

The clock was ticking. They hadn't paid the rent in months. In a few days the landlord would have the Marshall throw Lucy and her family out of their apartment, and her manager was ready to fire her because she had yet to sell a house. They might or might not receive more money for her husband's disability, but they didn't know when. Still Lucy went to work every day, showing houses to all her clients, even the No-buys. And everyday she'd sit in her car and cry, wondering where they'd live and what they'd do.

A few days before she and her family were to be locked out of their apartment she went to work as usual. "I felt like I had a huge, fifty-pound clock tied on to my neck, it was ticking away and there was no way to set it back." This particular day she was taking a No-buy to see houses, even though she and the other salespeople had already shown him forty-two. Lucy described the eight houses she had on her list to the No-buy. He dismissed five of them immediately, he didn't even want to see them. He agreed to see the remaining three, so they got in her car and drove off. As they drove toward the first house he told her he didn't like the neighborhood, he didn't want to see the house. He refused to even get out of the car and look at the second because he thought the roof looked like it needed repair.

"All I could think about was that I was going to be homeless. Tom, the girls and I were going to be living out of our car. That fifty-pound clock tied to my neck was ticking away," she later said. "Then, when we drove up to the last house and he smiled, I just started crying. I knew I finally sold a house."

The No-buy took a quick look at the house, which was exactly what he wanted, a replica of his boyhood home. He took out his checkbook, put down a deposit, and closed the deal without dickering.

"I cried when he signed the offer," Lucy said. "Even though we still didn't have any money, I knew we were OK. My philosophy was right, I succeeded because I stuck to it."

Lucy wouldn't get her commission until the escrow closed but she said it didn't matter. She said that if she could sell a house to a No-buy, she could sell to anyone. Brimming with confidence, she convinced the landlord to let them stay. Her manager was so pleased she had sold a house to a No-buy that he stopped threatening to fire her and actually began to help her, steering clients her way and otherwise assisting. That was the start of a successful, money-making career that led to their buying their first fixer-upper and beginning their real estate empire.

Lucy didn't make the sale to the No-buy because she was better than the other salespeople. She just knew how to stick to it. No, I take it back. She *was* better than the other salespeople, because she knew how to stick to it.

THE MAN WHO FAILED HIS WAY TO THE TOP

*"Failure is the opportunity to begin
again more intelligently."*
—Henry Ford

One of the most interesting men I ever met told me that he failed his way all the way to the top, mostly by accident. John was a middle-class mid-western high schooler who wanted to be a pole vaulter. His hero was Bob Richards, the famous Olympic pentathlete, winner of two gold medals, who appeared in flight on Wheaties boxes for many years. John was not a very good pole vaulter. He never got more than seven or eight feet off the ground, and he tended to land on his head. But he never gave up, he kept sprinting down the lane, the pole at his side, trying to soar over the bar. John did not master the pole vault, but the coach liked the way he sprinted down the lane, so he talked John into running the 100 yard dash. John became a pretty good sprinter—not the best, not an Olympic champion, but pretty good. John earned a Varsity letter and ran in the City championships. He didn't get what he originally wanted—he got something just as good.

In college, John wanted to be a high-powered courtroom lawyer, a Clarence Darrow or Perry Mason shouting objections, stunning the jury as he made the witness confess, dramatically pointing and shouting "No! *That's* the guilty man!" Unfortunately, John did not get good grades in his pre-law college studies. In fact, he made the Dean's *other* list. But he knew he was smart, he knew he could have done well. This self-knowledge lead him to reevaluate his goals. Did he really want to be an attorney, or was that the goal his father had set for him? John's failure (poor grades) turned into victory when he realized that he really wanted to be a businessman, not an attorney, and he switched majors. He didn't get what he thought he wanted—he discovered what he really wanted.

His first job out of college was as a salesman. He was given a list of customers to see regularly, including some very difficult ones. He only did a little better than average, but his cheerful demeanor in the face of repeated rejection impressed his boss. John's refusal to give up eventually lead to his racking up impressive sales, plus being promoted rapidly up the corporate ladder. He didn't let failure stop him—and he did better than expected.

In an attempt to move up even quicker, John once developed an innovative new sales approach for his company, which he boldly presented to the corporate officers at a meeting. This was a pretty daring move which led to disaster: they hated his plan, and they chewed him to pieces. The officers did, however, comment that they liked the way he spoke, and they complimented his graphs and charts. Years before, back in high school, John had been on the speech team. He had practiced and practiced, but never finished higher than third place in any tournament. Now his sales plan was a failure, but he left the meeting with a new, better job as head of company Public Relations and Communication. Failure didn't stop him—skills he struggled with twenty years ago were put to good use.

Some years later, as the Director of Development of a major firm, he oversaw the birth of a new computer program. It was a total flop. They couldn't sell any. The company had invested a lot of money in this project, and failure was going to hurt badly. Rather than give up, John thought about his problem for days. Then he realized that they didn't really understand their program and what it could do. As a result, they were trying to market the program to the wrong kind of buyers. John sent the programmers and marketing people back to work. Soon they had a stronger program. They had a better understanding of what their program could do, and who they should try to sell it to. The revamped program was successful. John got what he wanted—because he looked at the problem a new way.

READING FAILURE

"Adversity reveals genius. . ."
—Horace

"As kids," John would say, "we're taught how to read English, how to read maps, how to read music. But we never learn how to read failure. The word 'failure' rarely means 'finished,' 'it's over,' 'forget it,' 'you're done'. 'Failure' is one of those words that has many meanings. You have to know how to read it."

John will quickly tell you that his life was filled with failure. But he got to the top anyway, because he knew that failure was nothing more than a message—a message that could be read different ways. John kept going because he always found a positive interpretation of the message.

How do you "read" failure? What does failure mean? It could mean:

• *You're giving up too soon*—like I did with the bullies. An apprentice jockey named Eddie Accaro got off to a terrible start—losing his first forty-five races. He kept getting back on the horse, however, and retired as one of the most successful jockies in horse racing history, with 4,779 victories to his credit.

• *You have the wrong approach*—like John did with the computer program.

• *You're doing the wrong thing*—you're pole vaulting when you should be sprinting. The late Branch Rickey was not a very good baseball player. As a catcher, he was supposed to prevent the other team from stealing bases. In one game he played, the other team stole a record-high thirteen bases. No, he wasn't a very good player, but he later earned fame as a baseball General Manager, the man with the guts to bring the first black ballplayer into the major leagues.

• *You have talents that have not yet been developed*—more study or practice will put you on the road to success.

• *You need a rest*—come back when we're stronger. The withdrawal from Dunkirk in World War II kept the British Army alive to fight again.

• *You should examine your motives*—make sure you're doing what you really want to do, not what others say you should.

• *You should remember that you're only human.*

Through life, I've found that failure is usually success in a different form. As Thoreau said, a weed is really a flower whose beauty has not yet been discovered. So is failure often an overlooked opportunity for success. Failure can be many things. If we learn how to read failure, we can usually move on.

HOW DO *YOU* READ FAILURE?

*"We are constantly faced with great opportunities
brilliantly disguised as insoluble problems."*
　　　　　　　　　　　　　—Anonymous

How would you respond to these situations?

　1. Two people are laid off from work. They each have little savings, big mortgage payments, and a family to support.
　One says: *"I'm finished."*
　The others says: *"The job wasn't what I really wanted, so now I can get a better one."*

Who do you think will get back on their feet sooner?

　2. Two people are stuck at a boring lecture.
　One says: *"I hate these boring lectures! My whole day is ruined!"*
　The other says: *"This is pretty boring, I think I'll take a nap."*

Who do you think will leave the lecture in a bad mood and wind up fighting with their spouse?

　3. Two people can't find a job.
　One says: *"There is no good job out there for me. I might as well forget it."*
　The other says: *"There must be something wrong with my resume. Or maybe I'm not coming across right at the interviews. Or maybe I'm looking for the wrong kind of job."*

Who do you think will eventually get a good job?

　4. Two guys have their proposal at work turned down.

One says: *"I keep striking out. I'll probably get fired for this."*
The other says: *"Let's see, how can I fix this thing up?"*

Who do you think will eventually get a promotion?

THE FAILURES HALL OF FAME

"We're all failures—at least, the best of us are."
—James M. Barrie

Let's hear it for failure! Let's hear it, that is for people who don't let failure stand in their way. Let's hear it for those who refused to give up. Some of the greatest figures in history have been magnificent failures. If we were to make up a "Failures Hall of Fame," we would include:

Christopher Columbus, who set out to find a sea-route to India. He didn't get to where he wanted to go, he never realized he wasn't there, and he didn't know that his plan could not have gotten him there.

Mel Blanc, the fabulous voice of Bugs Bunny and many other cartoon characters. His story, as recounted to me by a friend, is a study in sticking to it. Hoping to be in the "voice" business, Mel went to Warner Brothers to demonstrate his voices. Unfortunately, the guy in charge refused to even hear Mel's voices. He was told to go away. Two weeks later Mel was back, and again he was told to go away. This went on and on, every two weeks for a year, without Mel ever getting a chance to demonstrate his voices. A whole year of rejection went by until one day, right on schedule, Mel knocked on the same door, expecting to be told to go away. This time, however, a new man opened the door. When Mel asked if he could demonstrate his voices the new guy said yes, and the rest is history. Mel Blanc was an incredible talent, but without his perseverance, Bugs Bunny would not sound like Bugs Bunny.

George Washington, the great general who seldom won a battle. In fact, his military skill was considered suspect by many of his contemporaries. Thomas Jefferson tactfully said that Washington was "not a great tactician." The more outspoken John Adams referred to General Washington as a "muttonhead" of a general. But Washington won the war. He kept the rag-tag army going until circumstances and the French combined to set America free.

Paul Erlich, who was looking for a cure for syphilis in the first decade of this century. He found one, called salvarsan, on his 606th try. A mere 605 failures didn't stop him. By the way, his 605 failures were so well-known, the successful drug was often called "606."

Thomas Edison, who failed over one thousand times in his search for a filament for light bulb. If Edison hadn't stuck to it, he would not have turned night into day.

Albert Einstein, one of whose teachers said that whatever the boy did when he grew up, he would do poorly.

Charles Goodyear, who ruined both his family's finances and his health as he struggled for years to make rubber useable. Although he had promised his wife, according to the story, to stop experimenting, he was using their kitchen as a laboratory while she was out. Surprised when she returned home unexpectedly, he hid his latest concoction in the stove, which was still hot. When she left he opened the stove to discover that the stove's heat had "cooked" his latest mixture into vulcanized rubber—exactly what he was looking for.

Some serious scientists, who were trying to invent a substitute for rubber during World War II. Along the way they accidently mixed boric acid with silicone oil. The mixture failed, it was not the rubber substitute they were looking for. Their accidental invention, however, later gained fame as Silly

Putty.

The Marx Brothers, who came into their own after plenty of failure. In fact, it was when an audience in Texas walked out on them and Groucho began insulting the audience that the Marx Brothers began to develop their distinctive style.

Nathan Birnbaum, a bad vaudeville comic who was thrown out of one theatre after another. The managers wouldn't hire Nathan after they saw him perform. He had to keep changing his name in order to get jobs. But he refused to give up. He finally teamed up with Gracie Allen and changed his name to **George Burns.** Now, in his nineties, George is still going strong.

Clark Gable, a wash-out in a studio film test because his ears were too big.

Lucille Ball, one of whose early drama teachers told her to try another profession—any other profession.

Marilyn Monroe, who was advised by an executive in the modeling industry to get a job as a secretary, because she'd never make it as a model.

Clint Eastwood, who was told by an executive at Universal Pictures to forget about being an actor because he spoke too slowly and his Adam's apple stuck out.

Jimmy Durante, who had a nose that would keep anybody out of show business. Rather than let it stop him, he turned his nose into an asset. Calling himself the "Schnoz," he made jokes about his nose, and went to the top.

The Beatles, whom Decca Records turned down early in their career, saying: "We don't like their sound." As the Beatles embarked on their first American tour, the head of Capitol Records, which was distributing their records in the U.S., said he didn't think Beatles records would be very popular.

Elvis Presley, who was fired after one performance at the Grand Ole Opry. The manager of the Opry, who fired Presley, suggested he go back to truck driving.

Pëtr Ilich Tchaikovsky, who suffered from terrible self-confidence. His teachers rarely gave him the credit he deserved. His first symphony was described as being "immature." The ballet dancers at the first performance of his Swan Lake were not up to par, and the show received very poor reviews. He often composed music that was very difficult to play, so it was performed poorly and poorly received. But he persevered and, in his 40s and 50s, he was a popular composer. Today he's considered one of the greatest composers of the 19th century, if not of all time.

Harry Truman, who failed in business and went into politics, becoming part of the Pendergast machine in Missouri. It's said that Franklin D. Roosevelt accepted Truman as his Vice-President in 1944 primarily because Truman was inoffensive. During the 1948 Presidential election campaign, everyone *knew* that Dewey would beat Truman. But Harry refused to give up. Instead, he gave them hell.

Brigadier General Billy Mitchell, who believed that airplanes would revolutionize warfare. Few supported him, but he persisted. In 1921 he had a crazy idea: He wanted to use airplanes to sink battleships. Everybody who was anybody lined up to say that it was impossible. The Secretary of the Navy said Mitchell should give up soldiering and write dime novels. Franklin D. Roosevelt, a former Assistant Secretary of the Navy, said it was "highly unlikely" that even a fleet of airplanes could sink a battleship. Newton Baker, the Secretary of War, was so sure Mitchell was wrong, he volunteered to stand on the ship while Mitchell tried to sink it. Luckily for Baker he stood somewhere else, because the bombers sent the battleship down to Davy Jones' Locker. Many of the great naval battles of World War II, including Pearl Harbor were not fought between ships: It was airplane against boat, just as Mitchell had envisioned.

Scientist Robert H. Goddard, whom the *New York Times* accused of not knowing high-school mathematics. Few people took Goddard and his rocket experiments seriously. Referring to one of his plans, the editors of Scientific American said it was not even worth considering. The Army Air Corp refused to work with him. Today, however, Goddard is considered the father of American rocketry. The Apollo space ship that took our astronauts to the moon was the descendent of his early rockets.

Chester F. Carlson, whose idea for a way to save a lot of effort in offices across the country was turned down by over twenty major businesses in the 1930s and 1940s. His parents were not wealthy, he had to work his way through college, the Depression was raging, but Chester wouldn't give up on his idea. Working and studying at night, he failed again and again to perfect his idea. He also endured continued rejection, finally selling a major chunk of his future earnings for three thousand dollars. Even then, years passed before his invention, called xerography, was brought to the market. By the way, his idea was finally developed and marketed by a struggling company called Haloid, which later changed its name to Xerox. Chester's idea, of course, was for what we now know as the Xerox machine.

Baseball pitcher Cy Young, who holds the record for most career losses (313). While he was losing all those games, he also set the record for the most career *victories*—511. Baseball's top award for pitching, the Cy Young Award, is named after this record-breaking loser.

Hank Aaron, the unhappy holder of the Major League Baseball record for hitting into the most double plays. He also holds the record for most home runs (755).

Ty Cobb, the baseball player who for decades held the single-season record for being thrown out while trying to steal a base. For many decades he also held the record for most stolen bases.

The unsung heros, the many people who succeed in learning, business, and in their personal lives because they won't give up. The small store owner who works sixty hours a week in good times and bad. The artist who struggles for years. The students who study twice as hard as their peers. The little kids who are determined to master baseball or ballet. All the people who know that failure is just another landmark on the road to success.

You, for sticking it out.

R$_x$: STICKITIVITUITY

> *"When nothing seems to help, I go and look at a stone cutter hammering away at his rock perhaps a hundred times without as much as a crack showing in it. Yet at the hundred and first blow it will split in two, and I know it was not that blow that did it—but all that had gone before."*
> —Jacob Riis

John, the man who failed his way to the top, told me that "If you want to succeed, you've got to have stickitivituity."

Stickitivituity (stick-i-tiv-i-tuity): the ability to stick to the task, no matter how long or difficult it may be. The "failures" in our Hall of Fame succeeded because they wouldn't, they *couldn't* give up. I guess that's what makes people successful: They *can't* give up. They want something so much, nothing will be allowed to stand in their way.

Most of the great men and women we admire had stickitivituity. They wanted something, and wanted it badly. That desire carried them to the top. What is it that you want so much that you'd allow nothing to prevent you from having it? Love? Joy? Knowledge? A certain job or income? Seeing your idea brought to fruition? A dream coming true? What is it that you *can't* give up on?

John has an interesting ritual he performs every day. "I don't always know where I'm headed," he says, "but wherever it is, I'm going to stick to it. Whatever I do, I do it with sticki-tivituity."

To remind himself to stick to it, while sitting at his desk he rolls some scotch tape into a ball and lets it stick to his fingers. He shakes his hand and wiggles his fingers, but the tape sticks fast.

"I often do this while I'm planning my goals or my next move. Perseverance is so important, even if I haven't begun yet, even if I don't know what the goal is, I keep telling myself to stick to it. I'm like the tape. I don't let go."

Let's learn a lesson from John, a man who knows how to read failure, and has "failed" his way to the top because he didn't know how to give up. It's important to have long- and short-term goals, yes, for we must know where we are headed. But it's equally important to *know that we're going to get there*, to know that once we start we're not going to stop. We're like the tape, we have stickitivituity.

Roll up a little ball of tape everyday, stick it on to your fingers. Shake your hand, see how the tape sticks fast. As you do so say:

> *Going over, under, around or through,*
> *Going swiftly or slowly,*
> *Going boldly or with caution,*
> *Going alone or among others,*
> *I'll get where I'm going*
> *If I just keep going.*

Chance does not determine our destiny. It's a matter of choice. Most of the people who succeed, whether it be in business, sports, education or their personal life, do so because they don't take "no" for an answer. I have built a pharmaceutical business and three medical practices from scratch. I know nothing about business, and I made more mistakes than I care to remember. The secret to *my* success, and, I believe, the secret to your coming success is:

1. *Hard work;*
2. *A good product or service; and*
3. *Stickitivituity.*

President Calvin Coolidge, "Silent Cal," knew this, pointing out that while the world is filled with educated, intelligent, talented people who never go anywhere, the halls of success are peopled by those who wouldn't—*couldn't*—give up.

And remember, as the famous singer Eddie Cantor said, it can take twenty years to become an overnight success. *Stickitivituity* will get you through your brief "overnight."

CHAPTER EIGHT

I COMMAND

*"The mind is its own place, and in itself can make
a heaven of Hell, or a hell of Heaven."*
—John Milton

In 1961, I was a young consultant in Internal Medicine and Cardiology. My specialty was diagnosing the tough cases. My dream was to set the medical world on fire with my brilliant diagnoses. I was going to be the best. I was going to diagnose diseases that hadn't even been invented yet.

I had already had one of my dreams come true: I had a beautiful young wife and four children, the oldest of whom was seven. I also had a few things that were not quite the stuff of dreams: an old car, a new house with a big mortgage, lots of bills, and few patients.

Yes, I had big dreams. I also had few financial resources to support my family and I. Big dreams, few resources and plenty of responsibility: That's the stuff of which high anxiety is born.

To become known to the other doctors, and to make some money, I drove all over the place. I'd see a patient anytime, anywhere. One afternoon I was excited to get two calls: One to see a patient in Long Beach, the other to examine a patient in Glendale. Long Beach was thirty or so miles south of Los Angeles, and Glendale was to the north. It was five o'clock. Although traffic back then was not as bad as it is today, it was still a force to be reckoned with. The idea of driving down to Long Beach then back to Glendale was crazy, but I really wanted the job—both jobs.

Traffic was heavy as I started down the road to Long Beach. Everyone in Los Angeles seemed to be on the road that day, all of them right in front of me, driving as slow as it was possible to go. I wanted to impress the doctors in Long Beach, I wanted to be on time, cool and confident, making a quick yet brilliant diagnosis that would save the patient's life. Then I'd zip up to Glendale and perform equally well. But all these cars were in front of me!

As I drove, or rather, as I crept along, I kept telling myself that things were bad, and getting worse: "This damn traffic! I won't make it, they're going to get someone else. Why do I always get stuck in traffic? Why did I come to Los Angeles? Why didn't I go back to South Philly where they don't have this traffic which is ruining my life?"

Soon I could feel my heart pounding, and it hurt. The front part of my head was throbbing. I was sweating. Naturally, my car did not have air conditioning and its clattering sound seemed to beat in cadence with my heart, making me more nervous. My hands gripped the wheel tightly. Pain shot through the upper part of my stomach as thoughts of, "I'll never get there. My career is over." stomped through my head.

Suddenly, it was too much. I pulled over to the side of the road. My heart was pounding away. Pain gripped my chest, stomach, neck, arms and back. I was panting as if I had just sprinted up ten flights of stairs. What was happening to me?

Suddenly and intuitively I realized what I had to do. I began talking out loud to myself. "Arnie," I said, "Slow yourself down. Slow down your breathing. Relax. Calm yourself. It will be all right. Let's see if you can slow your heart rate. Your life, or career, does not depend on this one case. If you don't make it, there'll be another one."

My pulse was dancing frantically at 150 per minute—too fast. I talked calmly to myself, took slow deep breaths, told my muscles to relax. Pretty soon I began feeling better. My heart rate fell to 100, then to 70, as my breathing slowed. My neck, back and arms loosened up. The pounding in my chest faded away. My stomach stopped barking. I stopped perspiring.

"Wow," I said out loud to myself, amazed at what had occurred. "I feel good."

Just then a puzzled motorcycle policeman poked his head through the open window of my car to ask "What are you doing?"

"I'm talking to myself," I replied.

"Are you OK?"

I explained to him what happened, how I apparently "thought myself sick," then cured myself with a "shot" of positive self-talk.

"Does it work?"

"It sure did for me," I replied.

"OK, doc," he said as he waved good-bye. "My job gets to me a lot, so I'll try it."

My positive pep-talk brought me out of an anxiety attack. We didn't know much about "stress" or positive thinking back then, but I marveled at how easy it was to talk myself in, then out, of distress. I wondered what, if any, would be the long-term effects of my heart, stomach and other parts of my body. Determined to avoid another anxiety attack, I called the Long Beach hospital. The nurse told me that the patient was resting comfortably, there was no need to rush down. If fact, she suggested I stop and have dinner until the worst of the traffic had passed.

I still had to do the consultation in Long Beach, then drive back past Los Angeles to Glendale Hospital, and I still knew that at best, I'd get home in the early hours of the morning. But I knew I could handle it. I felt good. I felt confident. I felt like I was going to set the medical world on fire.

Positive thoughts, actively applied, were the cure for

distress produced by negative thoughts.

WHEN THOUGHTS ARE "GERMS"

Macbeth: *"Canst thou not minister to a mind diseas'd,*
Pluck from the memory a rooted sorrow,
Raze out the written troubles of the brain,
And with some sweet oblivious antidote
Cleanse the stuff'd bosom of that perilous stuff
Which weighs upon the heart?

Doctor: *"Therein the patient must minister to himself."*

What had happened? Were my symptoms all psycholog-ical, in my head? Did I "cure" myself by fooling myself? No. My FUDfull[1] thoughts produced definite and dangerous phys-iologic, biochemical changes in my body. My symptoms faded quickly. Others are not so fortunate. As a physician, I have seen many people suffering from deleterious effects of long-term stress and negative thinking. Many studies support the link between negative thoughts and physical distress. Friedman and his co-workers focused on diseases such as Coronary Heart Disease (CHD), Peptic Ulcer Disease (PUD), asthma, arthritis and headaches. In their review of over one hundred investigations,[2] they noted that depression, hostility, anger and anxiety played a significant part in the development of these diseases—especially depression.

Many workers find their minds filled with FUD and other negative thoughts when they are stressed by chronic over-work, role conflict and harassment. It is well-known that with ongoing stress (negativity), there is an outpouring of corti-sones (the glucocorticoids from the adrenal gland), leading to

[1]FUD, as you remember, stands for Fear, Uncertainty and Doubt.
[2]Friedman, HS & Booth-Keinley, S.: The "Disease-Prone" Personality. Health Psychology 42:539-555,1988.

a drop in the amount and the abilities of important immune-system cells such as monocytes, macrophages and lymphocytes (the "big guns" of our immune system). Ongoing stress, with its accompanying depression, pessimism, hopelessness and helplessness, hampers the ability of the immune system "cell eaters" (phagocytes) to "eat up" invading organisms and cancer cells.[3] Stress can also reduce the actual number of the cells[4] all over the body. The big cells (alveolar macrophages) protecting your lungs are impaired by stress.[5]

Negative-thinking people tend to get recurrent colds, coughs, bronchitis, lung infections and other problems associated with a weakened immune system. (Triggered over and over again, bronchitis can lead to asthma-like symptoms. Thus, chronic disease is structurally present as a result of negativity.) Think of the incredible numbers of prescriptions we doctors write for antibiotics, the sprays, drops and other remedies used.

From head to toe, your body is at the mercy of your negative thoughts. That's the bad news. The good news is, from head to toe, your good thoughts can be a healing medicine.

Prescriptions for Health—or Disease

Driving down to Long Beach, I dwelled upon certain (negative) thoughts I thought were my own. These thoughts were mine, but not necessarily of my choosing, not entirely. You see, I was responding to the countless injunctions that had accumulated in my head since I was born. An injunction is a command, an order. When our teacher said to us, "You boys

---

[3] Gotjamason: *Alterations in reticuloendothelial organ structure and function following cortisol administration to mice.* RES, Jour. of Reticuloendothel. Soc. 8:421-433, 1970.
[4] Fauci, AS.: *Corticosteriods and circulating lymphocytes.* Transplant. Proc. 7137-40, 1975.
[5] Hunninghake, GW & Fauci, AS: *Immunologic Reactivity of the Lung.* Jour. Immunol. 118:146-150, 1977.

should quit school and become garbage collectors," that was an injunction. When they laughed at me for wanting to be a doctor, that was an injunction. When they described in such rich detail all the reasons I would never make it, that was an injunction. In my case, all those injunctions boiled down to pretty much the same thing: You won't make it. You can't do it. You're a failure. When I fell victim to the anxiety attack while driving to Long Beach, I wasn't simply responding to the fact that I would be late. *I was reacting to decades worth of injunctions, thousands of "failure" messages.* The possibility that I might be too late to wow the doctors in Long Beach turned into, in my mind, an unmitigated disaster, proof that I was an absolute failure. I was suffering from an injunction attack, a thought-crisis that lashed out at my physical health.

Injunctions are powerful messages "written" into our minds. We all have them, there's no escaping. What we think today, what we "write" into our minds, is always read by the light of yesterday's injunctions. How we respond to today's events, large and small, is powerfully influenced by our injunctions. What we think of ourselves, the way we treat others is colored by those same commands. Our response to others is based less on what they say and do than on our injunctions, or previous "programming." If our injunctions tell us that we're a failure, odds are that we will find a way to snatch defeat from the jaws of an impending success.

Driving down to Long Beach, I responded to the traffic with the full force of my negative injunctions. But injunctions need not be negative and harmful. They can just as easily be positive thoughts that lead to positive actions. My parents smiled proudly when I told them I was going to be a doctor when I grew up: That was a positive injunction. My Grandfather said that he and I together would graduate from medical school: That was also a positive injunction, one that swept aside many of the difficulties that are a routine part of medical training.

Our thoughts are prescriptions that we write for ourselves. Are you ordering health and happiness, or disease and distress?

The 5 Virtues

Our message in this book can be boiled down to this simple idea: *PTPA = Positive Thoughts, Positive Action.* If negative injunctions stand in your way, replace them with positive commands that will get you back on the PTPA track. It only takes thirty to sixty days to begin changing our thinking, altering the way we respond to events. Once we take control of our responses, we have control over our lives.

We've talked a lot about positive thoughts and positive action. We've given you two types of action: "Inner" action to help build belief in yourself, and "outer" action to accomplish a goal. "Inner" actions, with their affirmations, are very important, for they help you build belief in your ability to accomplish your goals. "Inner" actions also help you bury those negative injunctions which stand in your way under mountains of positive commands that will spur you to great "outer" action.

I tell my patients that the best way to overcome the negativity of the past is by adopting what Barry and I call the 5 virtues.[6] A summation of all the positive thoughts one can think, the 5 Virtues are really positive injunctions you give to yourself. They are: *Enthusiasm, Belief, Love, Forgiveness and Perseverance.*

I tell my patients to give themselves a daily spiritual transfusion of the 5 Virtues five times a day: Before breakfast, before lunch, during mid-afternoon, before dinner and at bedtime. I instruct them to recite these injunctions for the 5 Virtues, to see them in their mind's eye as they say them, and

6We first described the Five Virtues in our book, *Wake Up! You're Alive,* Health Communications, Deerfield Beach, FL, 1988.

to feel them with all their heart.

For **Enthusiasm**—*"I feel very enthusiastic today, I act enthusiastically toward everyone I meet."*

For **Love**—*"I feel strong love for myself and for all my fellow creatures. I respect and love everyone, even those I disagree with. Though I may regret the sin, I love the sinner. I love God/my higher power. I honor and love all those who went before me to make my way smoother. I love those who make my todays so sweet."*

For **Belief**—*"I strongly believe that I can conquer the unconquerable as I march to the top, easily handling each NICE [7] occasion that arises."*

For **Forgiveness**—*"I hereby forgive myself for any wrongdoing I might have done, being careful to make full restitution. I also forgive everyone for any ills they have done to me. Forgiving myself and others, I am free to go forward, doing the things I want to do, having the things I want to have, and being the good, compassionate person I really want to be. I am now free!"*

For **Perseverance**—*"With 'stickitivituity' as my slogan, I will persevere in all things I start, carrying them through to the end. I will do all the good that I can do. I will treat everyone with loving kindness because it is the right thing to do."*

We humans do pretty much what we're told to do. That is, we see today's events and respond based in large part of what has been "programmed" into our heads since we were born. Since the process never stops, it's never too late to stuff your head full of the positive commands that will spur you on to positive thoughts and positive action.

Just imagine that you can wake up feeling great, wide

[7]NICE = New, Interesting, Challenging, Experience

awake, with plenty of enthusiasm, belief, endorphins and energy, instead of feeling groggy, hung over, apprehensive and negative about what the day will bring you. Imagine stepping into a crisis with confidence. Imagine being able to finally set aside the grudges you've been carrying around for so many years. Imagine being able to talk heart-to-heart with your spouse and children. Add the 5 Virtues to your list of daily "inner" actions, make the Virtues and the "inner" actions in this book a part of your life. They will become first, your thoughts, then your words, then your actions, then your habits, and then your character. It's all automatic. They will be your injunctions, your *positive* injunctions. Instead of seeing everything through a filter of negativity, you'll look upon a life illuminated by joy and confidence as you go beyond positive thinking.

It's never too late to start, and now is always the best time to begin.

A Winning Injunction

Many people give themselves winning instructions, though they may not realize what they're doing. The other night,[8] there was a brief news story about a young woman named Patty Shannenberg. As a little girl, Patty fell in love with horses and jumping. Renting horses until she got her own, she taught herself how to guide horses through courses full of obstacles the powerful animals leapt over. She said she knew from the start that this was what she wanted to do, and she wanted to do it well.

Her dream of being a champion jumper turned into a nightmare when her back was shattered in a riding accident in August of 1977. She's been in a wheelchair since.

The news story showed Patty at the gym, in her wheelchair, lifting weights. Patty said something very powerful to the interviewer: She explained that just because you can't do something the old way anymore doesn't mean you have to give up. "There's always another way to do it," she said.

Patty has a new goal. She dreams of being a champion skier, a seemingly impossible dream for a woman confined to a wheelchair. But remember, just because you can't do something the way you used to, doesn't mean you have to give up. Having studied at the Big Bear Handicapped Ski School, Patty plans to try out for the U.S. Disabled Ski Team. There she was on television skiing down a mountain on a special handicapped ski device. She found a new way.

"There's always another way to do it." That's a powerful injunction, a tremendously positive command that propelled Patty to great positive action. Remember the man in the first chapter who could do 9,000 things? He and Patty are cut from the same mold. As the little news clip ended Patty said, "You're born with ten thousand things you can do." And even in a wheelchair, she insisted, you can still do eight or nine thousand things.

Positive thoughts, positive action.

THE PRESENT IS NO EXCUSE

"The people who get on in this world are the people
who get up and look for the circumstances they want,
and, if they can't find them, make them."
—George Bernard Shaw

"That's very nice, very inspiring," a friend said when we told him about Patty. "But if she had her own horse, she must have been rich. It's easy to be positive when you're rich."

Having been both rich and poor, I can tell you that there is absolutely no correlation between money and positivity. I can also tell you that many people beat poverty with their great injunctions, with positive thinking and positive action.

Soccer great **Pele** (born Edson Arantes do Nascimento), who led Brazil to the World Cup in 1958, 1962 and 1970, was born in a poor Brazilian village. A cobbler's son, this unschooled child who polished shoes made it to the top. A poor start did not stop Pele.

Jesse Owens (James Cleveland Owens) picked cotton in the fields at age seven, standing alongside his sharecropping father. A poor boy on a collision course with nowhere, won four gold medals at the 1936 Olympics. On one day in 1935, he set three world records and tied a fourth, all within an hour. One of those records stood until 1975. Lack of opportunity did not stop Jesse Owens.

Walter Reed, born to a poor, circuit-riding preacher, saved uncounted lives by discovering the cause of the dreaded Yellow Fever. The government named Walter Reed Army Hospital after this man who set his sights high.

Eddie Rickenbacker, whose father was a railroad laborer and died when Eddie was in grade school, quit school to take a job at age thirteen. He told the boss he was fourteen in order to get the job. He worked twelve hours a day, six days a week in a glass factory, then moved on to other jobs. Eddie became a car mechanic, and by age seventeen was in charge of research at the Frayer-Miller Auto Company. Although Eddie did not take his first airplane flight until 1916, he became one of America's great flying aces a short time later in World War I. Lack of money and a father did not stop Eddie.

The only person who ever won two Oscars for a single performance in a movie had "good" reason to give up on life. **Harold Russell**, manager of the meat department in a chair store, volunteered for the Paratroopers during World War II. A hand grenade exploded while Master Sergeant Russell was holding it. Russell wound up in Walter Reed Hospital where he recovered, minus both his hands.

Fitted out with artificial limbs and hooks, Russell was undergoing rehabilitation when he was asked by the Surgeon General to play himself in a film titled *The Diary of a Sergeant*. A Hollywood director who saw the short film at a war rally put Russell into a movie he was making. Called *The Best Years of Our Lives*, the 1946 movie about three servicemen returning to civilian life was a big success. Come Oscar night, Russell was presented with a special Oscar for giving "hope and courage to fellow veterans." Then he stunned the assembled stars by winning a second Oscar for best supporting actor, beating out some of the top actors of the day. In his book, *A Victory in My Hands*, which has been translated into twenty languages, Russell points out that *"it's not what you've lost, but what you have left, that counts."* That's a powerful injunction.

Robert Clary, the actor best known for his role as "LeBeau" on TV's "Hogan's Heroes," was slated to die at an early age. The Nazis grabbed Clary when he was only sixteen years old, sending him to Auschwitz when the only question seemed to be whether he would die quickly or die slowly, but Clary survived. He attributes his survival to the fact that once a week, when they had a little time off from being slave-laborers, he would entertain his fellow inmates. "That's what saved me," he said. "That was my way of forgetting where I was."

His positive action pushed the poisonous reality out of his mind, even if only for a short while. And his positive action undoubtedly saved others by helping them smile, if only for a moment. What was his instruction to himself? That it was possible to put aside, if only for a moment, the horrible fact that he was in a concentration camp. He told himself that it was possible to be positive in the midst of disaster.

Strong injunctions lead to positive thinking, positive action.

We May Be Now . . .

I'm a big believer in the future. As far as I'm concerned, with PTPA, things will always be better. I remember well one of the poems I read in my Boy Scout manual way back in 1939, when I was only eleven years old. This poem was really an injunction that helped me override many of the negative commands I received from others. I recite this poem for young people who tell me they'll never get anywhere. I write it down and ask them to memorize it. It's called "The Comer," by Edgar Guest.

> He may be now an office boy,
> A messenger or a clerk.
> The smallest man in the employ,
> Of those who give him work.
> But if he works with willingness,
> And wears a cheerful grin,
> He's on the roadway to success,
> That chap is bound to win.
>
> No power can hold that fellow down,
> He'll leave them all behind.
> The higher paid who leer and frown,
> And tell him he is blind
> To do more than he is paid to do,
> And not to ever shirk.
> Who say at five o'clock
> I'm thru with miserable work.
>
> Not long he'll be an office boy,
> Employees quickly see,
> Who works because the task is joy,
> And not just for the fee.

And others too will help him climb
To heights of far success,
Wealth will be his, and fame, in time,
Who works with willingness.

Happiness and Mental Health

How about happiness and peace of mind, the greatest treasures we can possess? Is there a relationship between injunctions, positivity and happiness? If so, can we command ourselves to be happy?

Many studies have shown that happy, positive people tend to have good mental health. One hallmark of good mental health is the ability to entertain positive thoughts about yourself, rather than to dwell on your inadequacies.[9] Another sign of good mental health is the ability to keep moving toward your goals in life, despite the interruptions and stumbling blocks that others call failure. A third sign is the ability to keep going despite what others may say about you (that is, you don't need their approval or reassurance, you're a self-starter, you know what you want to do and you do it).

Positivity and happiness are separate threads so intertwined upon each other that they are, for all practical purposes, one and the same thing.

Happiness and the Love of Others

Not only are people who like themselves more likely to be mentally healthy, they are also more inclined to view others in a positive light, and to reach out to them. Carl Rogers[10] and

9 Jaboda, M: *Current Concepts of Positive Mental Health*, Basic Books, NY, 1958. And, Diener, E: *Subjective Well-Being*, Psych. Bull. 95:542-575, 1984.
10Rogers,Carl L., *Client-Centered Therapy, Its Current Practice, Implications and Theory*. Houghton Mifflin, Boston, 1951.

others have shown that positivity breeds positivity, and that positive people are more apt to help others. On the other hand, if you look carefully at those who make fun of or look down upon others, you will often find a person suffering from a great sense of inferiority, or terrible feelings of self-hate.

Positivity and happiness are the first steps. Love of others is the inevitable follow through.

Happiness and Success

Thinking makes most things in life so. Oh, I don't mean that we can turn a hunk of lead into gold by thinking, that's a matter for alchemists. We can, however, turn our leaden attitudes into diamonds, simply by thinking it so. As our attitudes go, so do our thoughts. As our thoughts change from bad to good, our health improves, for we stop zapping our body with powerful hormones and other substances produced by FUD and other negativities.

Studies have shown that alcoholics, for example, who were more optimistic about life in general had a much better chance to become abstainers following treatment than those who were in the pessimistic Negative Thought, Negative Action mode.[11] Simple optimism, a way of thinking, helps people turn their lives around by throwing off the cruel taskmaster that is addiction. Breaking an addiction is not an easy task; for many, it is the most difficult thing they will ever be called upon to do.

Getting Happy

Happiness, good mental health and love of others are tied together, but how does one become happy? Philosophers have debated the meaning of happiness for centuries, while

[11]Streak, S & Conye, JC: *Social Confirmation of Dysphoria: Shared and Private Reactions to Depression.* J. of Personality & Social Psych., 44:798-806, 1983.

psychologists have argued over the methods for decades. I
side with President Lincoln, who, as a young man, suffered
from depression. Lincoln pointed out that "A person is as
happy as they make up their mind to be."

Positive thoughts are the precursor to happiness, and
happiness puts us on the road to strong mental health, love
and success. Where does happiness come from? Within.
From our thoughts. From the 5 Virtues and other positive
commands we place in our minds. From our strong desire to
be happy.

R$_x$: I COMMAND

I used to have a patient, an executive named Theodore,
who liked to give orders. "I write memos ordering people
around all day," he explained. "But the one I like to order the
most is me."

What orders did he give himself? "Basically, I command
myself to be happy." Theodore carried a memo he had written
to himself, which said something to the effect of: "Your job
today is to remember that you are a good man, that you are
kind to your family and employees, and that you deserve to be
happy. Follow these instructions to the letter."

Let's all pretend we're memo-writing executives and give
ourselves an order. Get a pencil and paper, write out your
command, the positive injunction you want to be your guiding
light.

What should you command yourself to do? Be happy, be
positive, always think the best of yourself and others. There
are many variations on this theme. Here's a sample, based on
the memo I wrote to myself: "Your job today is to be happy,
because there's a lot to be happy about."

Mine is a simple command, but effective. This memo, this

injunction, helps counteract other, older, negative injunctions. I read my orders every day, and I always know what I'm supposed to do.

I have another "memo," a list of practical "outer" actions I can take everyday. I'm not sure where I got this list, who gave it to me, but I follow it to the best of my ability. Everyday I look for a chance to:

1. *Mend a quarrel.*
2. *Keep a promise.*
3. *Forget an old grudge.*
4. *Stand up for what I believe is right.*
5. *Thank someone.*
6. *Compliment someone.*
7. *Encourage someone.*
8. *Tell someone I love them.*
9. *Keep in contact with an old friend.*
10. *Replace a suspicion I might have with trust.*
11. *Sing a cheerful song.*
12. *Take a minute to think about how fortunate I am.*
13. *Dream a great dream.*

Become your own boss. Tell yourself exactly *what* you want to be—a positive person—and *how* you want to be—joyful. Keep listening to yourself. Couple your positive thoughts with positive action. Pretty soon you'll see a change.

A Life-Giving Injunction

In our last book[12] we told the story of a fellow named Doc Wiley who knew all about the power of thoughts and injunctions. And he knew how to couple positive thoughts with positive action. The story bears repeating.

[12] *Making Miracles.* Rodale Press. Emmaus, Pennsylvania, 1989.

Doc was a Western Union messenger boy, no one special. But he believed it was his purpose in life to deliver a little bit of joy and optimism to everyone. He carried a pocketful of little pieces of paper, on which he had written slogans: Words. Words like "Today is a great day!" and "Keep your chin up!" and "Pack up your troubles!" With time he delivered a message, he reached into his pocket and gave the person one of his slogans. To Doc every day was a great day, another chance to spread joy.

When World War II broke out Doc tried to enlist, but they told him to go away, he was too old to be in the Army. So he volunteered to work in a hospital. And work he did, carrying bedpans around, wheeling soldiers up and down the hallways, doing whatever he could. The hours were long and the work was hard but Doc didn't mind. He was serving his country.

Doc hurt, however, every time he had to roll another soldier off a bed onto a gurney, and push him down the hall. Every time he wheeled out another dead man, he wanted to cry. Doc didn't want another soldier to die, not a single one, but what could he do? He wasn't a doctor, he had no special skills, no knowledge, no training, no nothing, he was just a delivery boy, one who now delivered bodies as well as messages.

That's it! The messages! That's what Doc Wiley did best, and that's what he could do for the soldiers. He decided to go with his strength.

The next morning, when the soldiers on Doc's ward awoke, they saw a message painted on the wall. In big letters it said: "NO ONE DIES ON THIS WARD." Six little words, "No one dies on this ward." When the hospital administrators found out about this they were furious, they wanted to fire the Doc. But the doctors and nurses said, "Wait a minute, don't fire him. It sounds strange, but all the sick and wounded soldiers are sitting up in bed. They're laughing about it and making bets as to who will live the longest. They look better. Leave it up!"

"NO ONE DIES ON THIS WARD." Those six words remained. You know what? No one died. There was a magic to those words. Every new soldier brought into the ward was made to understand that they couldn't die. They *couldn't*, else they break the magic spell.

What began as a joke to most people became deadly serious. Everybody knew they must believe, they must make those words come true. And they did. The death rate in that ward plummeted. The soldiers came in with the same problems as before, yet they stayed alive.

It was nothing. It was words, it was paint on a wall but it was everything: *It was an idea.* An idea that every sick and wounded man on the ward took to heart. The doctors and nurses took it to heart as well. Their attitudes about the patients changed—improved. With everyone believing the best would happen, the best was all but assured. The thought was written into all their minds and spirits. The seed was planted. And the seed prospered.

Eventually someone died. Doc's words—his great idea—couldn't save all the soldiers' lives. But his words were still magic, for the soldiers never died at the same rate as before. Protected by Doc's great idea, his command, they were always healthier on his ward.

It was just words, but it was exactly what they needed.

Exactly what we *all* need.

CHAPTER NINE

AT THAT TIME . . .

"A time to weep, and a time to laugh;
A time to mourn, and a time to dance."
—Ecclesiastes 3:4

Note: *Although some of the case histories in this book involved myself, some Barry, and some both of us, for the sake of convenience we present them all through my voice. The following episode, however, will be told through Barry's voice, for he was Marty's friend.*

Last night I watched the news. There was the usual litany of disasters, the plane crash in Idaho, the actress murdered in her apartment, the baseball player who committed suicide. There was also an item about a 28-year old actor who had been killed the night before, an innocent bystander who became a victim of crime.

It seems that two armed robbers stole a car. The police chased after them, and soon the robbers and the police were racing through the streets at 70 miles an hour. The robbers ran a red light, striking two cars. The first car was damaged, but the driver was OK. The second car tumbled over and over, finally coming to rest upside down, its driver dead. The newscaster said that the robbers, who had been caught, were being charged with murder. Then they showed a picture of the young man who was killed. He was a nice-looking fellow, a trim little beard hugging his jaw, a Peter Pan "I'll never grow up" smile lighting his face, a twinkle in his eye.

It was the same kind of news item we've seen thousands of

times before, another story about a victim of crime. But this time it was different, *very* different for me. The man who had been killed was my friend, Marty. As I watched the report of his death, I was sitting at the kitchen table in his parent's home, the same table I had sat at before with Marty, talking with him about girls, movies, and other things guys talk about. With me in the kitchen, watching the news report, were Marty's brothers, his cousin, and other people I've known— well, it seems as if I've always known them.

I first met Marty and his family when Marty was about five years old. He was a friendly little kid with eyes that seemed to smile at you, to welcome you. But I was nine, and he was only five. Marty's older brother and I spent that day playing with our squirt guns, trying to ignore the little squirt who wanted to tag along.

I have a picture from my thirteenth birthday party. It shows my brothers and friends lined up by height next to me. Marty is down at the end of the line, nine years old but still small, looking almost as if he were still but five.

I watched Marty grow as the years passed, seeing him at parties, weddings, holidays, funerals and other occasions that brought all the families and friends together. I always thought that Marty's eyes were very expressive. They say that a person's eyes hold the secret to their soul, that if you want to know a person, look carefully into their eyes. Marty's eyes smiled a lot, they welcomed you, they laughed with you. I always looked forward to seeing his eyes smile at me.

We lost track of each other for a time, Marty and I, as I went off to college and graduate school. When I returned to Los Angeles, I ran into Marty at the gym. He had grown up, I almost didn't recognize him. But the eyes, those friendly eyes, told me who he was. We began working out together. At first I could lift more than he, but he was diligent, in no time at all he put me to shame. His eyes were always very serious when we worked out. We'd work out and then have lunch. We could talk about his dreams of being a great actor and mine of becoming a great writer. He would tell me about his classes and auditions. I would tell him of the stories I was working on. He would encourage me. I would encourage him. He was one of the few people who took my dreams seriously.

Later we both took up karate, although we studied different styles at different schools. We'd get together to practice. I would show him how I had been taught to kick. He would very seriously explain that such a kick would not work, I should kick the way he had been taught. Then he would show me something he had learned. I would say that it was all wrong, he had to do it the way I had been taught. We'd argue until it was time to eat, and to talk about girls, acting and writing.

Injuries forced me to give up karate and to stop lifting weights. I moved to Northern California where I lived atop a hill, surrounded by redwoods, writing my masterpiece. Marty stayed in Los Angeles, taking acting classes and auditioning for parts, trying to "make it" in show business. He played some minor roles now and then, this and that.

When I returned to Los Angeles, Marty was deeply involved in acting, as well as in karate. He had earned a brown belt, one step below black. I was very busy with my work, and for one reason or another we lost the intimacy we had once enjoyed. We were still friends, we still saw each other at parties, weddings, holidays and funerals. He still had those laughing, friendly eyes. He still had the jokes, and he was still everyone's friend.

I hadn't seen Marty for some months, not since his brother's wedding. When my mother called, very early yesterday morning, to tell me that Marty had been killed, I didn't want to think about it. I went back to bed. I knew I should call his parents, his brother, his cousins, those people

I'd known so long, but I couldn't.

I was angry that whole day. Angry that my friend had been killed. Angry because I knew the criminals who killed him felt no remorse. Angry because I knew they'd stand in court with their lawyers and say it wasn't their fault Marty was dead. They would blame the police for chasing them so fast. They would blame the car they stole, saying the brakes were no good. They would blame the city because there was a pothole in the street. They would blame anyone and say anything to get off. They wouldn't care about Marty at all.

We watched the news account of Marty's death, his brothers, his cousin, the others and me. We saw his car turned upside down. We saw him lying next to it, a blanket pulled up over his head. We saw his picture fill the television screen. We saw those laughing eyes.

We sat at that kitchen table a long time, talking about the good times we had had with Marty, the things we did together. I told them some things they didn't know about Marty, and they told me things I didn't know. I was no longer angry when I left. I was simply sad.

Marty's funeral is tomorrow. We'll cry, and afterwards we'll go to his parent's house. We'll talk about him some more, and we'll feel a little better. We'll look at the pictures of him all around the house, the pictures of the little squirt who wanted to play with us big boys, the pictures of the teenager who dreamed of being an actor, the pictures of the young man on the set, and the pictures of him at the parties, the weddings, the holidays and funerals we all attended. I will look at those bright eyes of his, now dark forever, and wonder how much light has gone from my own eyes.

At This Time. . .

That was not the first death Barry had experienced, nor was he the first to lose a friend. Twelve years ago—has it been that long?—my little girl, Barry's sister, died a sad death. Less than a year before that, my mother passed away. Since then more have gone; kids I played in the streets with, boys I earned merit badges with, buddies I studied with, parents I raised kids with, grandparents I swapped pictures with. Some I liked. Some I loved. Some I don't remember very well. Some I recall with photographic perfection across forty, fifty years. Each death was darkness doubled, for the light in my eyes dimmed when the light in their eyes died.

Back in December of 1990, when Barry and I had just finished the first draft of the first chapter for this book, I showed it to my good friend Stan. Stan is Marty's father. Stan offered to read and critique it, so I gave it to him. Three days later I received a short note from Stan that read, in part:

> *Arn,*
>
> *I am returning the first chapter of your manuscript but find it difficult to make any coherent observations. At this time, I'm not the right person to offer objective comments.*
>
> *Notwithstanding appearances and the truly pleasant times we spend together, I can't relate to anything "positive" while thinking about our loss; it's even difficult to read such material. It's like asking an amputee about the quality of new shoes.*

I knew exactly how Stan felt. In one sad year I had lost my mother, my daughter, and a good friend, a man who had been a teacher to all of my children. My positive thinking seemed to mock me then, seemed to laugh and say "Smile! The sun is always shining" even as I watched their graves filling with dirt.

Especially after my daughter's death, positive thinking seemed the cruelest of hoaxes. At that time, all I could think of was who to blame. At that time, lashing out was in some ways comforting, while looking inward was in every way terrifying.

At that time, I was so very far down. All I could do was look at what I had lost. Quite some time passed before I could take my own advice and look at the wonderful things—the family and friends—I still had. At that time, I was angry and bitter. It took a while to understand that those harsh feelings would not only make me ill or depressed, they would likely poison the good relationships I had.

At that time, it seems as if we have little control over our thoughts, and even less desire to control what we can. There are other times, too, when positive thinking is far from our minds. I've seen these times many times, watching as families crowded around the bed, sadly waiting for death.

What good are positive thoughts when we've lost a loved one? Their positive thoughts didn't save them. Our positive thoughts didn't keep them alive, and neither can they bring them back. I won't tell you that you must think positive thoughts, even as you bury your loved one. I won't tell you that if you put your mind to it, you can choose your thoughts, no matter how bad things are. I won't tell you that, because I couldn't do it. I will tell you, however, that during periods of hardship, time is the best medicine. Speaking as a man who has lost loved ones, and not as a doctor, I can tell you that while the sorrow is never completely buried, time does blunt its edge.

At that time, when the light in your eyes dims, let your late loved one shine in your heart with the light of a thousand suns.

At that time, when positive thoughts are as shoes to the legless, remember that we will never walk without our loved ones, for they live on in our hearts.

At that time, when sorrow stands time still, know that the

turning of time will dull the sting of sorrow; slowly perhaps, but surely indeed.

The Germ Called Sorrow

At that time of sorrow, why should we open ourselves to positive thoughts?

I remember listening, as a young boy, to the "old people" telling each other that so-and-so should cheer up already, that she had mourned long enough. If she doesn't let go of her sorrow, they said, she'll make herself sick. Back then, in the 1930s and the 1940s, before medicine became so thoroughly modern and scientific, we believed that you could "make" yourself sick from sorrow. The doctors, the older ones especially, believed as well. Later, in medical school, I learned that there is no germ called "sorrow," so sorrow could not make you sick. Thankfully, medical science has advanced far enough to just begin to tell us what our grandparents knew so well: *Sorrow can sometimes make us sick.* That is, sorrow itself does not make us ill. Rather, sorrow, loneliness, guilt and other unhappy thoughts associated with the loss of a loved one can make us more vulnerable to illness by weakening our immune system.

Like every parent, I would have given my life to save my daughter's. But now that she's gone, letting sorrow turn from a natural phase into a terrible germ serves no purpose. In fact, succumbing to sorrow would be counterproductive, for if I die now, she'll die again, she who lives lovingly in my memory. At your time of sorrow, live for your sake, and for their's.

Celebrations of Life

At that time of sorrow, as we wait for life to slip away from a loved one, or as we ourselves prepare to draw our last breath, why should we open ourselves to positive thoughts?

Thousands of years ago, Moses brought forth the Children of Israel from slavery. Today, Jewish people commemorate the Exodus during the holiday of Passover. The eight day celebration begins as the family gathers for the Sader, listening as the youngest child present asks the Four Questions. In answering, the father tells the story of a people's deliverance. It's a holiday rich in joy and symbolism, with all eyes on the father.

Today we know that this joyful celebration can actually keep Jewish men alive—for a little while. Back in 1988, two researchers tracked the death rate for Jewish men throughout the year. They found that the death rate fell significantly below expected just before Passover. After the festivities, the death rate rises significantly about the expected: The rise following Passover was equal to the fall proceeding the holiday. In other words, the death rate for Jewish men follows its normal course for most of the year, dips significantly just before Passover, jumps up right afterward, then settles back down to normal.

The researchers studied Passover because it was of interest to Jewish people, especially Jewish men. Passover is a joyful occasion—a family celebration that highlights the father. The weeks leading up to the holiday are filled with anticipation and preparation. With something to look forward to, something to be excited about, something to live for, some Jewish men lived longer than they "should" have, long enough to celebrate the holiday. By way of comparison, there was no significant fluctuation in the death rate in the non-Jewish control groups. .

Passover was also chosen because it falls at a slightly

different time each year. The fact that the holiday moves around the calendar makes it possible to separate the beneficial effects of Passover from regular monthly rises and falls in the death rate.

In 1990, results of a similar study appeared in the Journal of the American Medical Association. This time the researchers examined the death rate for elderly Chinese women before and after the Harvest Moon Festival. Chinese families are male-centered, but the Harvest Moon Festival places the ceremonial emphasis on older women. Like Passover, the Harvest Moon Festival travels about the calendar, allowing researchers to separate the effects of the holiday from the regular monthly ups and downs in mortality.

The results? The death rate for elderly Chinese women fell below expected right before the holiday, rose immediately after, then returned to normal. The increase after was roughly equivalent to the fall immediately before the holiday. This study, using a different holiday, a different time of the year, a different sex and a different genetic stock, confirmed the earlier findings: *If we have something to look forward, something we place great value on, something that places value on us, we can delay our death.* Indeed, some preliminary evidence suggests that looking forward to a birthday or other personally significant event can postpone death.

I'll Dance at Her Wedding

On a more personal note, Eleanor, a woman my wife, Hannah, and I have known since our teen years, was stricken with a fatal cancer. In and out of the hospital, Eleanor kept telling my wife that she wanted to live long enough to dance at our daughter Barbara's wedding. The cancer grew stronger every day. So did Eleanor's determination to live long enough to dance at our daughter's wedding. Eleanor's once-ample body shrank as the disease—and the "cure"—took their toll. Her hair fell out, sores appeared on her body. But on that happy day, Eleanor danced at our daughter's wedding. She was obviously ill, her make-up and wig couldn't hide her illness, but there she was, dressed to the hilt, dancing at our daughter's wedding.

Sorrow can weaken our immune system, while joyful anticipation can keep some of us alive a little bit longer; two good reasons to open ourselves to positive thoughts, even in times of sorrow. Not force-feed ourselves, not pretend to have joy we don't, not turn our backs on the natural grieving process, but simply open ourselves to positive thoughts. At that time of sorrow, keep the channels open.

The Saddest of Times, the Happiest of Times

At that time of sorrow, as we wait for life to slip away from a loved one, or as we ourselves prepare to draw our last breath, why should we open ourselves to positive thoughts?

Years ago, when my children were young, I was called several times to see an elderly man at his little, run-down home in Los Angeles. Although he was suffering from kidney failure and other problems, although he was weak and often in pain, he was a joyful man. And the family focused on the positive, even though they didn't know where the next rent check would come from, even though they knew their father/grandfather was dying. That's not to say that they weren't sad or that he was anything less than beloved; still, even under these difficult conditions, they focused on the positive as much as possible.

Many times I've gone to houses where people are dying. They're invariably quiet and dark, with a heaviness in the air you can almost touch. But this house was noisy, with little kids running in and out, even playing in the room where the old man sat uncomfortably in a chair.

I didn't ask, but one of the women there told me that "Papa" loved to watch his grandchildren play. "He came to this country so his children and grandchildren could have a better life," she said. "How can we make his last days better than to let him see that his grandchildren are free, and they're happy, and they play?" Her father agreed: "I'm dying, so I might as well die smiling, watching the children play."

Nobody knew about psychoneuroimmunology, the mind-body connection, back then. We hardly knew about the immune system. But it was clear that even if joy did not prolong this man's days, it certainly lightened and gladdened those he had left. At that time of sorrow, help make your loved one's last days as good as they can be.

Positive thoughts are not a panacea, not a cure-all. Like all medicines, positive thoughts have their limitations. But positive thoughts to the grieved are not like shoes to the legless. Rather, positive thoughts are to the grieved as shoes are to the weary. Sometime, not now, but sometime, we'll put the shoes on and begin to walk again.

R_x: AT THAT TIME. . .

Light always shines in the darkness, even the darkness brought on by the loss of a loved one. At that time, when lashing out seems more comforting than looking within, when we feel that the terrible darkness in the deceased's eyes has drawn the light from ours, let's lift our eyes to the light. We cannot force our eyes to glow with joy we do not feel, but we can look to the light. We can always look to the light, far away though it may seem.

Light your candle. Hold your hands to the sides of the

flame, close enough to feel a little bit of warmth (but not too close). Notice that the palms of your hands, facing the flame, are lit by the light. It's as if you hold the warmth of life in your hands. Look into your handful of light as you say:

At that time,
When sadness seems to shutter my soul,
When sorrow swiftly strangles my joy,
When darkness daily doubles its hold,

At that time,
When the eyes of my heart see but blackness,
When the ears of my soul hear but sorrow,
When the tongue of my spirit tastes but bitterness,

At that time,
I open my ears to the sounds of joy.
I spread my arms to the joy of love.
I turn my eyes to the love of light.
I ready my heart for the light of love.

At that time, holding this light of love in my hand,
I turn to the future, lit bright by the light of love past.

Bring Joy to the Living

At that time, when we wonder what joy is, and doubt that we will ever embrace it again, what can we do? What can we do, especially when our sorrow is mingled with fear and guilt?

In one of our previous books, Barry and I wrote about a trip I took to the cemetery to visit the graves of my parents, my daughter, Eleanor and another dear friend:

"As is my custom, I parked my car at the bottom of the

hill and walked to the top, visiting each grave in turn, remembering the deceased and the joy they had brought to the world—the joy they had brought to me.

"Usually I leave the cemetery feeling up, not down, because the realization that these people who meant so much to me have passed on is more than balanced by the memories of the love and good times we shared. That day, however, I walked to my car feeling lousy.

"I didn't want to drive away feeling bad, so I sat in my car and thought about all the good times I had shared with each of the deceased. Thinking of the good is an excellent way to drive the bad out of your mind, but that day it didn't do the trick. For some reason, I couldn't shake the blues.

"I refused to leave the cemetery feeling unhappy, so I purchased a brass polishing kit from the mortuary shop and trudged back up the hill. One by one I polished the grave markers, again thinking of the good times I had had with the deceased.

"Now I felt that I had done something positive for my loved ones. I felt good, and could get on with my day.

"Why was I feeling so low that day? Because I was afraid to face the future without these good people by my side. Because I was frightened of experiencing the death of another loved one. More than that, however, much more, it was because I was feeling guilty. What more could I have done for them when they were alive? What could I have done to enrich their lives? What things had I said to them in anger, or out of frustration? How often had I been so self-involved that I had overlooked their feelings, their needs?

"Afraid to face the future, too guilty to look back at the past, I was caught in a sad and uncomfortable present, feeling fearful, and especially guilty. Guilt is a powerful emotion, a harmful emotion that preys on our peace of mind, and, acting through the mind, on our body as well.

What can we do to protect ourselves? How can we make amends and alleviate our guilt?

"We can't make amends to the deceased, of course, but we can do good for the living. All the good you wanted to do for your loved ones who have passed away, do it for the living. All the joy you wish you had given, give it to the living. All the good things you wanted to say, say them to the living. And all the love you have for the deceased, give it to the living. Give it all, and more.

"Tell your loved ones—your spouse or significant other, your children, parents, friends—that you love them. Tell them today, tomorrow and every tomorrow—in word and in deed—that you love them.

"Be sure to look them in the eye when you tell them you love them. Touch them. Hold their hand, put your hand on their shoulder, put your arm around their shoulder. Let them feel the warmth of your love.

"Don't be afraid to give your love. Love isn't limited, like the money in a bank account. Love is infinite. The more you give, the more you'll have. You see, you're happy when you're loving. That happiness stimulates the release of endorphins and other bio-chemicals, that, in the right amounts, lift your mood. The happiness, the good feelings that result, help reduce your loneliness, fear, guilt and other negative feelings. When you love, and when you give your love, you put yourself into a positive feedback loop that benefits everyone. . .

"It seems as if I've gotten far afield, away from the guilt that day at the cemetery. But I really haven't. I was feeling guilty because I wasn't sure I had done everything possible to express my love for my loved ones when they were alive. I was wondering who else might die before I had a chance to demonstrate my love for them. For whom else would I feel guilty?

"I resolved that day never to feel that guilt again, for I would tell my loved ones that I loved them, in word and in deed, today, tomorrow, and every tomorrow for the rest of my life.

"So love the living. Honor the living, cherish the living, bring joy to the living, and you'll never feel the guilt I did, that day at the cemetery."

Yes, bring joy to the living. Bring joy to your living loved ones. Now go a step further, bring joy to people you don't know. How? There are many ways. Marty's parents joined *The Compassionate Friends*, an organization for parents who have lost a child. They joined looking for help, but found themselves giving comfort to other saddened parents. Simply by being there, they let others know that they were not alone in their sorrow. Simply by being there, they could say to others that they really *did* know how it felt. Simply by being there, they gave others a chance to cry without feeling ashamed, and a chance to laugh without feeling guilty. Simply by being there they brought joy to the living, to people they had only just met. What better way to honor one's memory than by bringing joy to the living? You needn't have any special wisdom or insights—just be there for them.

We can all honor our loved one's memory by bringing joy to the living. Or we can work to prevent another death like theirs. My youngest, Bruce, was supposed to drive to Northern California for a concert with a friend, Adam. For some reason Bruce didn't go. Adam's car was struck by a drunk driver and Adam was killed. If your loved one was killed by a drunk driver, join *Mother's Against Drunk Driving (MADD)*, bombard your Congressman and Senators with letters demanding tighter laws, speak out at civic organizations and schools. If, like millions more, your loved one was felled by a heart attack, crusade for better eating habits. We

know how to eliminate most heart disease, so you could
spread the word and keep one more person alive. If your cigarette smoking loved one was the victim of lung cancer, raise
hell with Congress for giving tobacco growers subsidies. Make
life miserable for the tobacco companies. Speak at elementary
schools. Convince one child not to start smoking. Honor the
deceased by keeping someone else alive—even if you never
know who that someone is.

Ease another person's sorrow by saving a life. And as you
bring joy to the living, remember that you are among the
living. Bring joy to the living, to yourself, by remembering all
the joy and love you once shared with the deceased. Wait, I
take that back. We did not *once* share joy and love with our
loved ones, for the love and joy lives on in our hearts. While
we grieve, as is natural, let's not turn our inner eyes away from
that love and joy inscribed on our hearts. Let's read of that
love, every day, through our tears. We shouldn't lock away our
good memories because they are accompanied by sadness.

Healing the Hole in Your Heart

Marty's mother, Miriam, wrote a letter to the judge who
was soon to pass sentence on the robbers who murdered
Marty. Describing her great love for her lost son, she said that
she felt as if a hole had been punched in her heart, as if her
soul had been ripped in two. She also wrote that Marty always
"gave people the hope that things can get better, and that there
is always tomorrow."

There are no more tomorrows for the deceased, but we
who live on can take comfort in the fact that time dulls the
edge of pain's sword. Marty knew that there is always
tomorrow. Even as we grieve for our loved ones lost, let's look
for tomorrow.

CHAPTER TEN

THE BEGINNING

"Happiness depends upon ourselves."
—Aristotle

Scientists at Vanderbilt University and the Weissmann Institute of Science in Israel have published a study propounding a new theory. They say that the human egg sends out a signal when it is ready to be fertilized. Upon receiving the signal, sperm which have been waiting patiently in "holding areas" continue the race toward the egg.

If that's true, it means that one of our first acts, even before life, is to send out a signal, calling forth that which we desire. Our life begins because we acted to bring to us the thing we want. Unfortunately, many of us lose the habit of telling the world what we want, knowing that we'll get it. Too many of us are content to accept what is tossed our way, hoping it will not be as bad as we fear it might be.

Let's go back to the beginning, back to telling the world what we want. But before we can do that, we must tell ourselves that we deserve the good things we want, knowing in our hearts that we are good and capable people. Not perfect, not infallible, for we are human, but good, capable, and most of all, deserving.

All this, we must believe. As an Internist and Cardiologist who has seen more suffering than I can remember, and as a scientist trained to identify and destroy disease, I can tell you with all my heart that the lack of "heart" is the greatest illness of our time. Lack of belief in ourselves, in our goodness, in our abilities and in our worth, has laid more of us low than any disease I know of. But the cure is where the illness is: In our thoughts, in our actions, in our spirit, in our "heart." We *can* be happy, if we choose to be. We *can* set ourselves on the road to success, if we choose to. The choice is ours.

I tell this to most everyone I meet. Many are incredulous: "You mean all I have to do is want to be happy?" they ask, amazed.

"That's not all, but it's the beginning," I answer. "Positive thoughts coupled with positive actions are the key to most everything in life. Develop the belief, then act on the belief that you are a good person, that you deserve the best.

"Let's go back to the beginning," I tell them. "Back to the first thing we ever did. Let's send a message. Let's call out for what we want."

Some people think I'm crazy, but others catch the spirit. They stand with me and say, out loud: "I want happiness! I want peace of mind! I want success!"

You know what? *I really works!* If I could bottle this and sell it by prescription only, I'd make a fortune. Yes, there are viruses and bacteria that attack the body, some of them quite serious. Yes, we suffer injuries that harm us dearly. Yes, we have little or no control over certain things in life. But we have the cure for the "thought germs" that attack our mind. We don't have to allow injuries to the body to ruin our happiness. And if we can't change life, we can change our attitude towards what happens to us. *That's* where our power lies—in our minds.

A Short Note

. . .about negativity. Many people will tell their doctors things they won't tell anyone else. I hear a lot of "confessions," plus plenty of "whys." "Whys" are the reasons people give to explain why they are or are not successful, are or are not rich, are or are not happy, are or are not married, and so on. I'd say that seventy to eighty percent of the "whys" I hear are negative: "I didn't get what I wanted because someone stole it from me." My parents wouldn't let me do it." 'The Asians/ Mexicans/Blacks/Whites/Locals/Immigrants took all the good jobs." That so-and-so Governor passed a law which keeps people like me down."

I cringe when I hear the negative "whys" recited, delivered with fervor and feeling. Taking a cue from President Lincoln, I tell these people, and constantly remind myself, that:

You cannot cure your poverty by tearing down the rich.
You cannot end your sadness by bad-mouthing the happy.
You cannot strengthen your will by denigrating the strong.
You cannot enlighten yourself by insulting the wise.
You cannot grow taller by tearing down others.
Negative thoughts are chains, tying you down.
Positive thoughts are as a light, leading you forward.

NTNA (negative thoughts and negative actions) is an invitation to mental distress, physical disease, and disaster in every part of life. There's more and more evidence of the dangers of NTNA every day. PTPA (positive thoughts and positive action) is always the best approach to life.

SUPER-DOOPER WRAP UP

> *"The beginning is half of every action."*
> —Greek Proverb

Barry and I finish up our seminars with what he jokingly calls our "Super-Dooper Wrap Up." I think he calls it that because I keep forgetting my lines and stepping on his, so he has a super-dooper difficult time trying to figure out what I'm going to say next.

We tell our audiences that the real failures in life have the best memories. They remember all the little hurts and troubles. The losers of the world know what they don't like to do. The winners have figured out what they like to do, and they go out and do it. The winners concentrate on getting out of their own way.

Speaking of winners, there's a man who went into a sea-food restaurant and he said to the waiter "Waiter, I love lobsters. I want the biggest lobster you have."

The waiter said "Yes sir," and came back with a big lobster. But the lobster was missing a claw.

So the man said to the waiter: "Waiter, this lobster is missing its claw! How come?"

The waiter replied: "Sir, this lobster was in a fight."

Angry, the man said: "Waiter, I don't want the loser! Bring me the winner!"

Successful people often fail miserably before they thrive. What is success? Success is the progressive realization toward a predetermined, worthwhile goal. In other words, success is simply finding a goal and working toward it. Speaking of goals, our favorite philosopher, Yogi Berra, said: *"If you don't know where you're going, you'll end up somewhere else."* Someone else, equally wise, said: *"If you don't know where you're going, how will you know when you get there?"*

There are plenty of people out there waiting for their ship to come in—but they never sent one out. Not only that, they're waiting at the airport. But the PTPA person, the positive thinking and positive acting person, knows that we should always couple our good thoughts with good action. The PTPA person sends his or her ship out, looking for adventure.

How do we reach our goals? First by belief. In the

Scriptures we are told: *"Whatsoever things you desire, when you pray, believe you receive them, and you shall have them."*

This passage is really talking about positive thoughts, affirmations, injunctions. Affirmations are undoubtedly one of the most important elements you can use to change your life. The words and ideas that run through our minds are very important. Most of the time we aren't consciously aware of this stream of thoughts, and yet what we are "telling ourselves" in our minds is the basis from which we form our experience with reality—the way we view our world. In other words, we really deal with other people not according to what they tell us, but according to what we've been telling ourselves.

So, if we change our perceptions, miracles can happen. We can change our life. The Scriptures tell us that the eye is the lamp of the body. So if our eye is sound, our whole being will be full of light. But if our eye is not sound, our whole being will be full of darkness. A negative outlook on life invites in the darkness of disease, depression, and death. The positive outlook on life, however, will draw in tremendous light, giving you health, happiness and success.

In other words, we should give our minds a strong idea, then act on that thought. If need be, we can take action, "inner" action, to help create belief. Our minds will respond, if we give it a chance.

A Spiritual Tune-Up

Doctors cannot cure 90% of our ailments, for these are problems of "thought disease," of psychoneuroimmunology, problems that begin with our negative thoughts and negative actions. The cure is to give ourselves a spiritual tune-up. Like any other engine, the human engine must be kept running smooth. How do we do this? With good eating, good exercise, good living and good thinking.

We must replace every weak thought with a strong one, every negative thought with a positive one, every hateful thought with a loving one, and every sad thought with a joyful one.

Are our thoughts so important? Well, our thoughts become our words, our words become our actions, our actions become our habits and our habits become our character. From thoughts to character, from thoughts to biochemistry, from thoughts to health or disease, the pathway is clear.

Marcus Aurelius wrote: *"A man's life is what his thoughts make of it."*

In Matthew we read: *"According to your belief is it done to you."* According to your belief of what? Your belief in yourself. People treat you according to the way you treat yourself.

Ralph Waldo Emerson, whose great essays changed the lives of many for the better came to the heart of the matter when he said: *"A (person) is what he thinks all day long."*

Maxwell Maltz, the plastic surgeon turned philosopher who noted that fixing a person's nose or skin did not make them happier if they felt ugly inside, said: *"If you keep your positive goal in mind and think of it in terms of accomplished, fact, you'll experience winning feelings."*

Napoleon Hill summed it up when he said: *"Anything the mind of man can conceive and believe, it can achieve."*

In Philippians we read:

> *Whatsover things are true,*
> *Whatsoever things are honest,*
> *Whatsoever things are just,*
> *Whatsoever things are pure,*
> *Whatsoever things are lovely,*
> *Whatsoever things are of good report,*
> *If there be any virtue, if there be any praise,*
> *Think on these things.*

Think on all these positive things. Say these things, see these things, feel these things coming true in your mind. Think on enthusiasm, belief, love, forgiveness, perseverance, and all the other great thoughts. Think on positive thoughts, and dream of the great, positive actions you will undertake. Think on these things, and make your life exactly what you want it to be.

Whatsoever things are positive, think on these things. Then take action.

SUGGESTED READING

Adams, George Matthew. *You Can.*

Amos, Jim. *Focus or Failure.*

Bartmann, Bill. *Billionaire: Secrets to Success.*

Blanchard, Ken. *The One Minute Entrepreneur.*

Fox, Arnold and Fox, Barry. *Beyond Positive Thinking.*
Making Miracles.
Wake Up! You're Alive.

Jones, Charlie "Tremendous". *Life is Tremendous.*

Kohe, J. Martin. *Your Greatest Power.*

Matheson, Mark. *Freedom From Fear.*

Mitchell-Halter, LuAn.
Leadership Lessons Learned By The Impossible Dreamer

Hill, Napoleon. *First Editions.*
Magic Ladder to Success.
Poems That Inspire You to Think and Grow Rich.
Wisdom of Andrew Carnegie. . .

Robert Cavett. *Success with People.*

Sanborn, Mark. *The Fred Factor.*

Stone, W. Clement. *Believe and Achieve.*
The Success System That Never Fails.

Mandino, Og. *A Treasury of Success Unlimited.*

Peale, Norman Vincent. *The Power of Positive Thinking.*